Murder & Crime

PENDLE
AND THE RIBBLE VALLEY

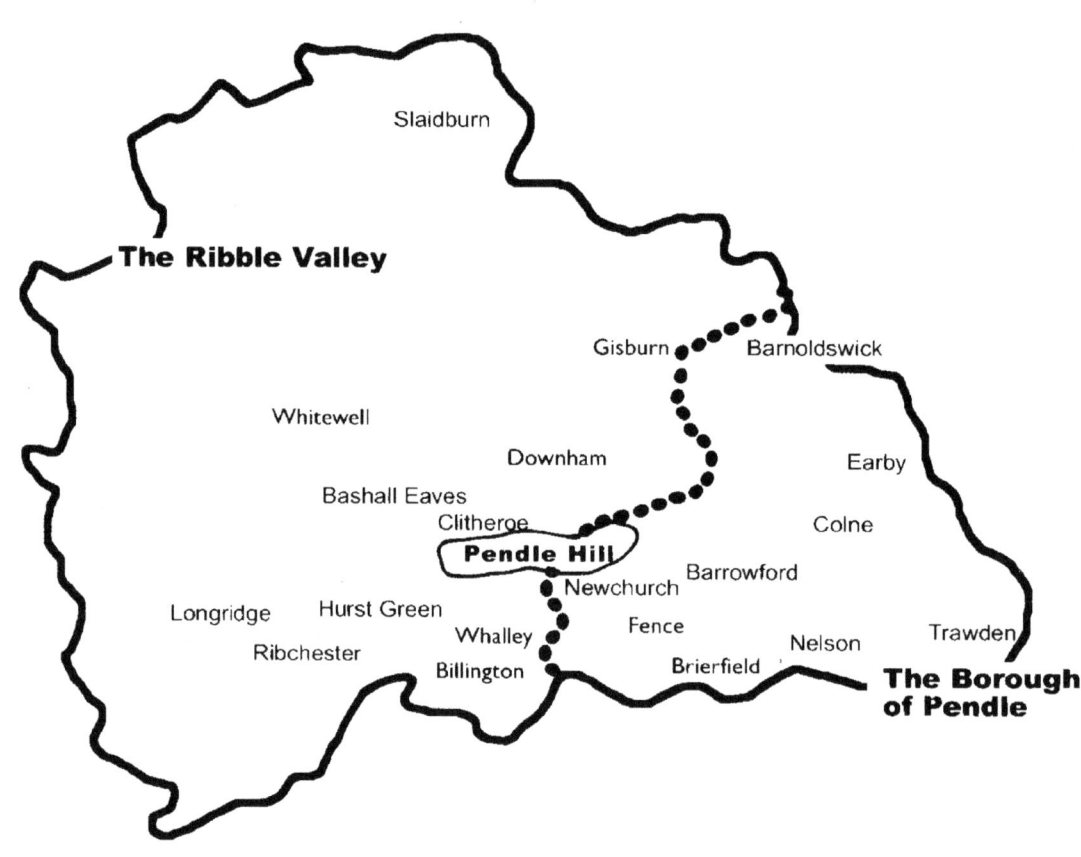

Murder & Crime

PENDLE
AND THE RIBBLE VALLEY

JACQUELINE DAVITT

Frontispiece: Map by Toby Lawrence.

First published 2007 by Tempus Publishing

Reprinted in 2015 by
The History Press
The Mill, Brimscombe Port
Stroud, Gloucestershire, GL5 2QG
www.thehistorypress.co.uk

© Jacqueline Davitt, 2007, 2015

The right of Jacqueline Davitt to be identified as the Author of this work has been asserted in accordance with the Copyrights, Designs and Patents Act 1988.

All rights reserved. No part of this book may be reprinted or reproduced or utilised in any form or by any electronic, mechanical or other means, now known or hereafter invented, including photocopying and recording, or in any information storage or retrieval system, without the permission in writing from the Publishers.

British Library Cataloguing in Publication Data.
A catalogue record for this book is available from the British Library.

ISBN 978 0 7524 4495 6

Typesetting and origination by Tempus Publishing
Printed in Great Britain

Contents

Acknowledgements 6

Introduction 7

Murder & Crime in Pendle and the Ribble Valley 8

Acknowledgements

With thanks to:

Christine Bradley, and the other Lancashire librarians who helped so willingly. Pat and Andy Catlow, Joan Coates, John Davitt, Kim Lawrence, Toby Lawrence, Phoebe Lomax, Jack and Dot Thompson, and also my editor Cate Ludlow for her advice and support. Special thanks to the local newspaper reporters of yesteryear, whose careful and interesting recording of events made this book possible.

Line drawings are by Kim Lawrence and photographs by the author, unless otherwise acknowledged.

Introduction

This book not only explores the murders and major crimes of Pendle and the Ribble Valley over many centuries, but also includes many lesser crimes that illustrate the social and moral circumstances in which they were committed. The harsh, and often barbaric, ways in which criminals were punished in days gone by contrasts sharply with today's 'softer' regime, and give us an insight into the lives of the people of past generations who moulded this unique area of the British Isles.

BARNOLDSWICK

This town, known locally as 'Barlick', was listed in the Domesday Book as Bernulfswick (meaning Bernulf's town.) Before the arrival of the canal, Barnoldswick was a small village, but the community grew along with the wool and cotton industries to become a good-sized town.

Unfit to Plead (1939)

By 1939, the courts were aware that people suffering from mental illness could not always be held accountable for their actions, as a report in the *Craven Herald* and *Pioneer* of 21 July, 1939 shows.

On 24 June of that year, Richard William Matthews, a quarry man in his fifties, attacked an old man at the Craven Lodging House, Barnoldswick, where they were both living. A deputy employed at the lodging house, thirty-nine-year-old William Taylor, had intervened to protect the eighty-year-old from his assailant. Matthews had then knocked them both to the ground, viciously kicking Taylor in his stomach, head and face. It was a brutal beating and Taylor died from his injuries, which included a broken skull, the next day.

When Matthews appeared in court at the West Riding Assizes, his defence lawyer presented a medical report, which he claimed showed that Matthews was unfit to plead because of insanity. The medical officer at Armley Prison gave evidence that he had kept the prisoner under constant observation in the prison hospital and was of the opinion that Matthews was 'of unsound mind.' His mental state had deteriorated whilst in custody to the point where he believed that people were poisoning him and pumping him full of noxious gases. The medical officer concluded that as the prisoner was suffering from 'delusional insanity', he would be unable to apprehend the course of the court proceedings, would be unable to challenge a juror, or to understand fully the evidence given against him.

The Assize judge, Mr Justice Tucker, addressed the court, saying: 'In this country we do not try people if they cannot understand and follow the proceedings or give instruction to counsel or possibly to take objection to any particular juror.' He added that it was his opinion that the jury should be satisfied with the medical evidence, and that they should find Matthews insane and therefore unfit to stand trial.

The jury consulted without retiring and gave just such a verdict, whereupon Mr Justice Tucker declared that Matthews should be 'kept in strict custody until his Majesty's pleasure shall be known.'

BARROWFORD

Barrowford is a linear village built down one side of Pendle Water with the park, home to the heritage centre, occupying most of the other side. The heritage centre, housed in Park Hill, was home to the Bannister family from the fifteenth century. They were the family from which Roger Bannister, the first man to run a four-minute mile, is descended.

The Lock-Up

Jesse Blakey, in his *Annals and Stories of Barrowford* (1929), describes the Barrowford lock-up of days gone by as a low building with a flagged roof, standing at the corner of The Square. It was a temporary jail where offenders arrested by the local constable remained securely overnight until they could be moved to Colne the following day.

Old Barrowford. (courtesy of Lancashire County Library and Information Services)

'Lovers' Tunnel', Barrowford park.

Blakey tells how, on one occasion, a tall muscular stonemason's labourer was in the lock-up for 'having had too much beer and talking too loudly'. During the night the man, who knew about methods of building construction because of his job, climbed onto a stool, forced a flag from the roof, climbed through, and went home to his wife. Blakey does not record what the consequences of this jailbreak were for the escapee, nor if the roof was further fortified to prevent others taking the same way back to their beds.

Police Murder (circa 1850-1860)

Jesse Blakey's book also contains a tale relating to the attack of two local constables near to where the Fleece Inn once stood at the centre of the village.

A man from a house near to the inn was roused at midnight by the sound of loud curses and heavy blows. He saw five or six men fighting, but could not see who they were in the blackness below his window. The next day he got up at daybreak and found several broken chair legs and wooden spindles lying in a pool of blood next to the heavily bludgeoned bodies of the two Barrowford 'bobbies'. Both were badly injured and one constable died shortly afterwards.

The murderers were never caught, but were thought to have been amongst the drinkers at the Fleece the previous night. Blakey mentions that suspicions fell on 'a bad character' who had left the village shortly after the incident and, rumour has it, confessed to the crime on his own deathbed.

The Fugitive (1897)

On the last Friday of February 1897, a warehouseman who lived and worked in Barrowford took a gun and shot his wife before turning the weapon on his spinster cousin.

Fred Nowell and his wife had a stormy marriage, reportedly due in the main to Nowell's unreasonable jealousy. On the day of the tragedy, Mrs Nowell had been to see a solicitor about getting a legal separation from her husband. Her husband's cousin, Miss Constance Nowell, had accompanied her and the two had just sat down for a cup of tea when Fred Nowell arrived home. He hung his coat in the passageway and after spending a few minutes in an adjoining room he approached his wife, asking her, 'What about the summons?' We do not have her reply, if she made one, but Nowell then locked all the doors and went to retrieve a revolver from his coat pocket. His wife, sensing something was seriously amiss, followed him into the passage where he turned upon her, firing directly towards her face. Mrs Nowell fell to the floor and her husband fired again.

Constance rushed to help the injured woman and Nowell fired at her as well. The bullet passed through Constance's hand as she raised it to protect herself, whereupon Nowell fired his last three bullets at his cousin. One hit her in the face, one grazed her shoulder, and the final one hit her breast. Somehow, the terrified girl found the strength to climb onto a chair, jump through the windowpane and run to the house next door.

Alerted by the gunshots and screams, several neighbours saw Nowell running across the field behind the row of houses, heading in the direction of Wheatley Lane, and although some of them gave chase, the fleeing man had too good a start for them to catch up with him. They were also somewhat fearful that he may still have the gun, but this was later found, empty, lying on the table at the murder scene.

Dr Pim arrived to pronounce Mrs Nowell dead from a bullet to the brain, but finding Constance still alive, he sought the help of Dr Cramp of Burnley and his new Rontgen X-ray equipment to locate the bullets fired into her. The two pioneering doctors found and extracted a bullet from her left jaw, but Miss Nowell's injuries proved too severe and she died a few days later.

The Fleece Inn.

The police, meanwhile, had issued a detailed description of the wanted man and although there were reported sightings of him at Gisburn and Hellifield they suspected that he may have gone abroad, as he had about £30 in his wallet and had previously expressed an interest in emigrating to Australia. He had been known to wear a false moustache and beard in order to follow his wife about, undetected, and the police feared he might have adopted this disguise in order to avoid capture. No trace of Nowell ever came to light and he never returned to claim his home or possessions.

Strange though it may seem to us today, a self-styled poet wrote and printed memorial cards to sell locally. The cards carried the following verses:

VERSES WRITTEN ON THE BARROWFORD TRAGEDY

Sad news alas we hear, in famed old Lancashire
While looking down the papers meets the eye
And scarcely one clear day now seems to pass away.

Barrowford police station c. 1950-60. (courtesy of Lancashire Library and Information Services)

E're violence claims its victim thus to die.
Of a murder we are told which makes the blood run cold
Poor Mrs Nowell she has lost her life.
At Barrowford they say on that fateful day
Then happened this cruel and tearful strife.

Chorus –
Mrs Nowell's gone her friends for her will mourn
In the prime of life it was hard to die
Her earthly face is o'er on a bright and happier shore
We hope her spirit it has gone on high.

It seems Nowell and his wife lived a very unhappy life
For frequent quarrels happened day by day
And throughout their married life their lot nothing else but strife
Which caused Mrs Nowell anguish and dismay.
But on that fateful day Nowell took his way
And into a shop we are told he went
And bought a revolver which was shown him over
And back home he went on cruel murder intent.

What could his motive be for this sad tragedy?
None at all, is what the people say
For not content with strife, he took away a life
That now lies sleeping in the silent clay
And the police are doing their best Nowell to arrest
But as yet no tidings of him can be found
And all around Burnley excitement it runs high
While they are searching for him all around.

Miss Nowell so they say is mending everyday
Of that we are all glad to hear
And every credit's due to the doctors who
To try and save her life they persevere
And may God in his love look down from above
So to sooth the pain of this dear one left
For while on her sick bed many tears she'll shed
While thinking of a dear one that's bereft.

BASHALL EAVES

This village, on the banks of the river Hodder, has had many name variations, such as Beckhalgh and Bakesalf, during its long history. Fifteenth-century Bashall Hall was once the home of the Talbot family, and the remains of John Halstead's early nineteenth-century corn mill are still standing.

A Very Cold Case (1934)

James Dawson, a middle-aged farmer, lived with his sisters and a nephew at Bashall Eaves. It was his habit to visit the Edisford Bridge Inn, about twenty minutes walk away, for a drink in the evenings. The evening of Sunday 19 March brought no change in this routine, although he did leave the hotel much earlier than usual.

As he made his way home along the dark country roads, a car drove past him and for a moment, he thought he saw a figure silhouetted against the hedgerow. He also noticed that one of his resident farmhands, Tom Kenyon, was in the car. A few seconds later, Dawson felt something hit his back. He thought somebody had thrown a stone at him but could not see anyone hanging about, so continued on his way. When he got home, the farmer ate his supper and when Tom Kenyon came in at about 11 p.m., they were heard having an argument. During the night, the pain in Dawson's back worsened and, when morning came, he found his bedclothes covered in blood. He asked his sister to see what the problem was: she found a gaping wound in his back so sent for the doctor.

After examining the farmer's wound, the GP called the police and ambulance services to the farm, and Dawson went reluctantly to hospital where the doctors x-rayed him. They found, and removed, a homemade bullet that seemed to be a filed-down piece of steel rod, perhaps a fireside poker. When the police interviewed him, the injured man denied that he had any idea who had shot him, or knew of anyone with reason to do so. He discharged himself, but when his condition deteriorated, he agreed to go into a Blackburn nursing home, where he died from septicaemia and gangrene, still unwilling or unable to offer any more information about his attack.

Edisford Bridge Inn.

The police, led by Detective Chief Superintendent Wilf Blacker from the West Riding force, questioned every local gun owner and searched every tool shed and workshop in the area for evidence as to where the murderous missile had come from, but to no avail. Blacker then summoned the entire community of Bashall Eaves to a meeting at the village hall, but no one offered any information whatsoever on that night, nor at any time else during the police investigation into James Dawson's murder. Calls for witnesses went unheeded, and despite dragging the nearby streams and rivers, no trace of a possible weapon was found.

In June 2005, the *Lancashire Evening Telegraph* carried an article entitled, 'Police reopen murder mystery seventy-one years on.' The story told how police were set to review the murder of James Dawson following the publication of a book, *The Wall of Silence*, written by the victim's great-niece, Jennifer Lee Cobham. It included details of the author's investigations.

The book alleged that new evidence had emerged, including details of an unusual gun found years ago in the barn next to the Bridge Inn where James had been drinking on the night of the shooting. The gun, which may have been a walking stick converted to fire bullets, had allegedly been sold and was thought to be in a private, untraceable gun collection. Mrs Cobham called for her great-uncle's killer to be finally unearthed, saying, 'After so many years my great-uncle Jim has ceased to be a flesh and blood person who had suffered horrible pain at the hands of a murderer', adding, 'solving the mystery once and for all would finally allow Jim to rest in peace.'

Inspector Bob Ford of Clitheroe police (now retired) gave a statement agreeing that the force had a duty to investigate any new facts or evidence, but added that the passing of time made inquiries to establish the facts very difficult. He did however confirm that the case would always remain open until it was resolved.

BILLINGTON

In AD 798, the Saxons battled around Whalley in an area known as Billangaho, from which the two neighbouring communities of Billington and Langho took their names.

Judge Walmesley (1537-1612)

Sir Thomas Walmesley's family home was Showley Hall, Clayton-le-Dale. He was the eldest of ten children and entered Lincoln's Inn in 1559, before being called to the Bar in 1567. He had the reputation of being an excellent lawyer, and received a knighthood in 1603. Around 1570, he married Anne Shuttleworth, buying the Dunkenhalgh estate in 1571, where he lived until his death in 1612. He served as a judge of common pleas during the reigns of Henry VIII, Edward VI, Queen Mary, Queen Elizabeth I, and James I.

Judge Walmesley was a well-known and respected figure on the local circuit. Said to have Catholic sympathies, he was not a man to conform to peer pressure, or to the opinions of others. An astute, sometimes tough, businessman, he invested heavily in buying land in his native Lancashire where he contributed to several local charities.

The courts of the time often took place in local inns, and the 'Judge Walmesley' at Billington was named after him. When he died at the age of seventy-five, over 2,000 mourners attended his funeral. He was buried at Blackburn, but Cromwell's men smashed his magnificent tomb to bits in 1625.

Retribution or Smoke Screen? (1839)

On Friday 20 December 1839, four poachers got into a confrontation with gamekeepers on land belonging to William Henry Hornby, esquire, at Billington. During the affray a gamekeeper,

The sign at the Judge Walmesley, Billington.

Thomas Isherwood, was shot dead. At the inquiry into his death, the jury returned a verdict of wilful murder and the search was on for the poachers, named as Adam Mercer, Joseph Crossley, Joseph Abbott, and James Parker.

About a week later, Adam Mercer, also known as Adam O'Cute, walked into the police station and surrendered himself to Mr Perris, the constable. He claimed that after the incident the poachers had fled towards Blackburn before separating about 2 miles away from the town. At this point, he had gone to Manchester with Abbott and had been unaware that Isherwood was dead until he returned to the area several days later. He was adamant that he had been opposed to the attack made on the keepers and had been bruised and battered during the scuffle. Mercer was admitted to the House of Correction for further questioning; meanwhile, the following notice appeared in the *Blackburn Standard* of 29 January 1840:

SIXTY POUNDS REWARD

Whereas John Crossley, Joseph Abbott, otherwise Yates, and James Parker, are charged (along with Adam Mercer, now in custody), with the wilful murder of Thomas Isherwood, Gamekeeper to William Henry Hornby, Esquire, at Billington, near Blackburn, in the night of Friday the 20th of December last;
NOTICE IS HEREBY GIVEN,
That a reward of £30 will be paid by the said William Henry Hornby on the apprehension and committal of the said John Crossley, and a reward of £15 on the apprehension and committal of the said Joseph Abbott or James Parker.
JOSEPH CROSSLEY is a native of Blackburn, a labourer, 30 years old, about 5 feet 4 inches high, light complexion, blue eyes, red hair and whiskers, broad set and has lost one of his upper front teeth; he usually wore a dark velveteen shooting coat, with large pockets and black buttons, baragon trowsers, and quarter boots.
JOSEPH ABBOTT, otherwise YATES, is also a native of Blackburn, a labourer in an iron foundry, 30 years old, about 5 feet 6 inches high, light complexion, blue eyes, sandy hair and rather long face; usually wore a dark velveteen shooting coat, with large pockets and black buttons, and baragon trowsers, much stained with oil.
JAMES PARKER, also known by the bye-names of CORNSHAW JEM, and TALLOW JEM, is a native of Icornshaw, near Crosshills, Yorkshire, a hand-loom calico weaver, about 30 years old, 5 feet 7 inches high, stout made, dark complexion, dark brown hair, grey eyes, rather long face, and has a mark on his right cheek from an old cut; usually wore a dark velvet shooting, with large pockets and black buttons, short moleskin trousers and waistcoat, and quarter boots.
It is particularly requested that any information which may lead to the apprehension of the above mentioned may be sent, as soon as possible, to Mr Robinson, solicitor: or to Mr Thomas Perris, police officer.

By November of the same year, hope had diminished of finding these wanted men but a letter from America was to end the search for the alleged ringleader, Joseph Crossley.

The letter, addressed to Mr Euin Marsden of Over Darwen and written by the recipient's son, contained a passage, which the *Blackburn Standard* of 25 November 1840 quoted verbatim:

A Mr Crosslow from Blackburn Penny Street came here in the spring from his own words shot the gamekeeper near Ribchester his trouble was so heavy that he could not live, he died in the poor house with nine days sickness and he wished often he had been shot instead of the keeper on his deathbed he proposed he saw the gamekeepers in the bushes and cried out they were coming they were coming for two days before his death his lips were seen to move he appeared to be talking and appeared to be sensible but no one could tell what he said.

The letter went on to tell how Crosslow (Crossley) had made his escape from England after shaving his beard and having a false tooth fitted at the front of his mouth. The writer of the article saw no reason to doubt the veracity of the letter and concluded, 'We see in the fate of this misguided man a startling instance of God's retributive justice.' Whether this was indeed the case, or Crossley had instigated the letter to cover his tracks is not known, but no more was heard about him – or his accomplices.

A Murderous Secret (1884)
When Mary Ann Seed and Sarah Coates, neighbours of Mary Anne Charnley of Old Roadside, Billington, realised that the young weaver was ill they sent word to Dr W.P. Counsellor of Whalley, who responded with a house call. On examining his patient, the doctor found that she had very recently given birth, but there was no sign of a child and Charnley denied that this was the case.

Dr Counsellor asked the two neighbours, who had waited downstairs, to see if they could find the baby or discover what had happened to it. The women did as asked, and found the body of a fully developed baby boy hidden under the cellar steps. He was wrapped in a blue apron and a piece of old sackcloth. The poor mite was not breathing and felt cold to the touch. Mrs Coates identified the apron as one that she had seen the lady of the house wearing, and a shocked Mrs Seed went upstairs to challenge Charnley, saying, 'Mary Anne, you brute, we have found the child.' She received no reply.

The women sent for the police, and when PC Wadeson arrived, he heard what they had to say and went up to the bedroom to be greeted by Charnley wailing, 'O Lord, have mercy on me!' When the policeman delivered a caution the stricken woman replied, 'I am sorry for it now. I am sorry I have done it. Why did I do it? O Lord, forgive me!'

On returning next day to examine the child's body, Dr Counsellor discovered that the face was discoloured and the nose crushed flat, whereupon he declared that the baby boy had been born alive and healthy, but had died as a result of quiet suffocation. The killer may have used a hand or bedclothes to cover the infant's nose and mouth.

The coroner at the inquest into the case, held at the Judge Walmesley Arms, said he was satisfied that Mary Anne Charnley was the child's mother and that he thought that the only conclusion the jury could reach was that the mother had taken the baby's life. After deliberating for almost an hour the jury returned a verdict of 'Wilful Murder' against Mary Anne Charnley.

BRIERFIELD

Brierfield lies on the road and canal between Nelson and Burnley and was a busy mill town in the heyday of king cotton. The weaving industry replaced coal mining when the seams, found in the nineteenth century, ran out. The town had strong links with the Quaker movement and the Friends' Meeting House still stands, just down the hill from the Marsden Cross.

Minor Crimes (1879)
Serious crime has not changed much over the centuries, but some minor offences, such as these recorded in *The Colne and Nelson Times* of Saturday 11 October 1879, no longer pop up in our

Quaker Meeting House, Brierfield.

modern judicial system. The following crimes all took place in Brierfield in one week, and the perpetrators faced the court at Colne Petty Sessions.

Tossing

Four youths named William Heyworth, Henry Jenkinson, George Mitson and Thomas Tunstill, were charged with 'tossing and making bets'. They were all found guilty, and Heyworth and Jenkinson fined five shillings each whilst Mitson and Tunstill had to cough up one shilling each.

Jumping on the Pavement

Edward Barlow and Joseph Holt, both Brierfield men, were charged with 'jumping on the pavement', whilst sixteen other men faced a charge of 'congregating on the footpath watching the jump'. This 'sporting' event took place at about 7 a.m. on a Sunday morning, and involved Barlow and Holt stripping down to their underpants and pumps (plimsolls) on the street. The two then jumped, using iron bars and weights, whilst the referee, Robert Wright, took bets on the prowess of the jumpers.

Unfortunately for them, a police constable witnessed their shenanigans, and the 'sportsmen' were fined twenty shillings each and the gamblers fined sums between five and fifteen shillings, depending on their previous records.

Vagrancy

Frederick Hopkinson, described as a 'professional beggar', faced a charge of 'begging from door to door' in the town. He was discharged after promising to leave Brierfield and not return.

The Runaway Rate Collector (1908)

In 1908, the rate collector for Brierfield Urban District Council was a Blackpool man, John Ainsworth Eckersley. The sixty-six-year-old was also an assistant overseer for the poor of the town and was generally well thought of and respected. However, his reputation became somewhat tarnished when investigations by the council uncovered considerable defalcations in both the money received by him as an overseer and moneys received in his role of rate collector, and the councillors obtained a warrant against him. He was also summoned to appear at Preston Bankruptcy Court on 15 November 1909, but failed to turn up. He had last been seen on 13 November, when he left Brierfield, stating that he was going to the station to catch a train to his Blackpool home.

Further investigations revealed that the rate collector had been living far above his means. He owned a comfortable house on Station Road, Southshore, Blackpool, where his elegant household furniture was valued at £400 – a princely sum at the time. He also owned a motor car worth about £200 and held an interest in a Blackpool sweet business, the stock there worth a further £80. Brierfield Council put in a claim to the official receiver for £2,500, which had gone astray under Eckersley's administration, whilst the overseers of the poor in the town claimed that £1,714 15s 6d, also Eckersley's responsibility, had similarly gone missing. Money was also due for an oil painting of his daughter that he had commissioned and for other lavish items.

Mrs Eckersley declared that the assets such as the house, car and furniture did in fact belong to her personally, whilst the debts owing were those of her missing husband. The bankruptcy hearing was adjourned until further notice when, hopefully, John Ainsworth Eckersley would have returned to face the music.

Burning at the Stake

There are records of burning at the stake as a punishment as far back in history as the thirteenth century, although the practice probably began many years before. It was used to dispose of heretics of both sexes, but later mostly became the fate of women found guilty of crimes such as treason, coining (melting down clippings of coins to make counterfeit currency), and witchcraft. Burning was a punishment favoured by Mary Tudor who, during her five-year reign, ordered the deaths of over 200 heretics who refused to turn from the Protestant faith.

Victims of this punishment were usually either tied to a stake before being surrounded by wood that was then set alight, or were chained to a stake to dangle over a mound of burning wood and debris.

After 1700, women sentenced to death by fire were first strangled by a rope, before their lifeless bodies were burnt.

CLITHEROE

Clitheroe has long been a market town, central to life in the mainly rural Ribble Valley. Its ancient castle keep sits on a massive limestone outcrop, which dominates the high street and now houses a museum.

Clitheroe.

The Vanishing Cadaver (1773)

George Battersby, by trade a carpenter, took up cattle dealing in his later years. He was sixty years old in 1773 when he travelled from his home in Slaidburn to sell meat at Clitheroe fair. During the day's trading, he had an argument about prices with three men – Henry Worswick, Dr Herd and Nicholas Wilkinson – and he was packing up to leave as night fell when the three men returned and laid into him, according to a local man, James Nowell, who was just leaving a nearby public house and went to help Battersby.

Nowell forced the attackers to release their victim, standing guard whilst the injured man removed the handkerchief they had stuffed into his mouth and another they had tied round his neck, only leaving him when he thought the coast was clear and it was safe to do so. However, other witnesses saw Wilkinson run into his house – and re-emerge carrying a club and a knife. Together with his accomplices, he was seen heading in the direction that Battersby had just taken.

The following morning, James Nowell claimed that he had come upon Battersby's beaten body, lying in a pond, whilst out for a walk. As he stood surveying the scene, Dr Herd appeared and began to wash blood from stepping stones which crossed the stream. Nowell hid until Herd had finished his task, and then went to tell his brother what had transpired before returning to keep an eye on the body. A few hours later he saw Herd, Worswick, and Wilkinson remove the body, whereupon he went to seek help.

Although the police carried out their enquiries on receiving Nowell's information, they did not find a body and there was not enough evidence of murder to warrant a trial at the time.

Three years later, in 1776, a group of schoolboys found a footless body in Clitheroe bone house. Some flesh and hair still clung to the cadaver, and medical opinion was that it was Battersby's body, which had been stored in lime since death, thus explaining its condition. For years, there had been a pile of lime in the churchyard where the bone house stood. However, Dr Herd, who had quoted the lowest price for its removal and got the job, had recently removed it. Herd subsequently stood trial for Battersby's murder, along with Worswick and Wilkinson.

Their defence tried to implicate James Nowell in the killing, saying that his evidence now differed from his statement made at the time. They also called a witness, a servant named Francis Turner, who testified that Nowell had been in bed at the time he claimed he had found the body in the pond. The defence belittled the medical view that the body dumped in the bone house was Battersby's, going on to question whether George Battersby was dead at all. They put forward a theory that Battersby was still alive, and may have conspired with Nowell to fake his own murder so that he could disappear, taking his debts along with him.

The trial judge declared that he was satisfied that the body was that of George Battersby, but left it to the jury to decide whether or not Nowell's evidence held water. The jury returned a 'not guilty' verdict on Herd, Worswick and Wilkinson as they felt the case had not been proved beyond doubt, but the townsfolk of Clitheroe had already decided on their guilt and ostracised the three men.

The Great Abduction Case (1891)

On a bright sunny Sunday in March 1891, the parishioners of St Mary's church noticed a strange carriage outside the church gate as they left the morning service to stroll home. The occupants of the carriage did not show themselves until the churchyard was almost empty, but when Mrs Emily Jackson, and her sister, Mrs Baldwin, stepped out onto the street three men leapt out of its depths and approached the two ladies. Mrs Jackson was surprised when one of the men proved to be her husband, Edmund Haughton Jackson, with whom she had not lived since their wedding day over three years earlier.

Edmund took his wife by the arm and urged her to get into the carriage. When she refused, he took hold of her waist and dragged her towards it. Emily struggled whilst her sister clung

The gateway of St Mary's church, Clitheroe.

on to her arm and the mêlée culminated in the married couple landing in a heap together on the carriage floor. Mr Dixon Robinson, who, along with Dr W.H. Robinson of Clitheroe, was accompanying Mr Jackson, took hold of Emily's protruding feet, lifted them inside and slammed the door. The horses set off at a rattling pace and Mrs Baldwin fainted.

At about 2 p.m. that afternoon the carriage arrived in Rover Street, Blackburn, drawing up at No. 2, Jackson's home. The door was immediately thrown open by the maid to admit the dishevelled party; an hour later, Emily's brother-in-law arrived with his son but was denied admittance. Mr Baldwin then communicated with Chief Constable Lewis at the central police station, who refused to interfere as it was a domestic matter, whereupon Baldwin and his son headed back to Clitheroe to obtain warrants against the three men for assault on Mrs Baldwin during the abduction. Armed with the warrants, Baldwin returned to Rover Street, where a crowd was now gathering as news of the abduction spread. He asked the police to break into the house to serve the papers and, when they refused, threatened to do so himself. They strongly advised him against this illegal act and he had no option but to stand with the throng and watch for signs of his sister-in-law.

Monday morning found the house in a state of siege. The blinds and curtains were firmly drawn whilst newspapers, milk and grocery deliveries were taken in by means of a rope and basket let down from a bedroom window. Meanwhile, the chief constable of Clitheroe was holding negotiations with the abductors, finally reaching an agreement that the men would present themselves at Clitheroe police court on Wednesday 11 March on condition that the force withdraw without serving the warrant.

True to their word, Jackson, Robinson and Robinson arrived at the court in readiness to answer the assault charge. The defence wanted to know why the warrant had been issued, but not served, on the Monday. The prosecution failed to come up with an acceptable answer, so the case was adjourned until 23 March. Before this could happen, however, a writ of *habeus corpus* was applied for on behalf of Mrs Jackson to compel her husband to bring her to the court to be freed. Mr Justice Cave dismissed the application, judging that Jackson had a right to keep his wife with him, especially as he had obtained a decree for restitution of marital rights in July

1889. Next day, however, the court of appeal overturned the decision on the grounds that Mrs Jackson's confinement constituted cruelty, and Mrs Jackson left the court by the judges' entrance, where a police escort led her to meet her waiting relatives.

Edmund Haughton Jackson was dismayed by this decision and, feeling that he had been badly served and represented by his wife, her family, and the courts, he went on to write a book that gave his version of events. The book was published as *The True Story of the Clitheroe Abduction; OR Why I Ran away with my Wife!* It was edited by W.H. Burnett, managing editor of the *Lancashire Evening Express* and *Blackburn Standard*, and sold well.

Jackson begins his narrative by describing his 'old style romance' of his wife, whom he met whilst picnicking with friends at Sawley. At first, she declined his marriage proposals. Jackson gave up hope and began making arrangements to set up a farm in New Zealand, but after a chance meeting with Emily she wrote to him to arrange a secret meeting. They recommenced 'courting' and eventually married in a low-key ceremony at St Paul's church, Blackburn, on 5 November 1887. They then went to Emily's family home at Shaw Bridge to inform them what they had done. Emily stayed the night to 'smooth things over' whilst Edmund returned to Blackburn to finalise the travel plans. When they met up the next day Emily told him she would not be going to New Zealand with him as planned, but would follow later. Jackson offered to delay the trip, but she was adamant – so he set off forthwith.

Many letters passed between the couple in the coming months, with Emily's words becoming colder and Edmund's replies becoming hotter and angrier as it became clear that she would not be joining him. There were also financial accusations levelled against him, and his wife made it clear in more than one missive that she, and her family, thought Edmund had married her for her money – which she vowed he would not get. Jackson returned to England in 1889, but Emily refused to see him, or to leave her family's home. Edmund blamed her relatives for this estrangement, and he was convinced that if the two of them could reunite as man and wife, they would be able to resolve their differences. To this end, he applied for, and got, a decree for restitution of marital rights. The decree made no difference to Emily's attitude so, in desperation and with the feeling of right on his side, he recruited Dixon Robinson and Dr W.H. Robinson and hatched his abduction plan.

In a closing chapter of his book, an unrepentant Jackson damns his wife thus: 'Good wives before now in thousands have given up all to be true and loyal to the man of their choice. She has given up nothing. She has made no sacrifice. Her marriage vow remains as false as a dicer's oath.'

Skeleton Discovered (1907)

The discovery of a human skeleton at the Salt Hill quarry in 1907 caused great excitement among the local population, with crowds of onlookers making their way to the site to satisfy their curiosity. Quarry workers found the skeleton at a depth of about 3ft during routine excavations and, apart from a broken skull, it was remarkably well preserved. Strangely, a stone weighing about 2cwt covered the skeleton's chest area, as if it had been placed there for burial. The large size of the remains gave rise to a theory that they may be prehistoric but this hypothesis was discounted by an eminent professor of the time.

Never a Wrong Word (1919)

In 1861, the Offences Against the Person Act made it illegal to supply or use 'any poison or other noxious thing' or to use 'any instrument or other means' to cause a woman to miscarry a child. It further outlawed abortion by either the woman herself or any other person such as a doctor, nurse or pharmacist. This did not stop some pregnant women seeking 'remedies' or backstreet abortions, but anyone undergoing, or aiding and abetting in any way, such an act could be tried for crimes up to and including murder. The act was enforceable until the 1967 Abortion Act came into being.

When Alice Jane Derbyshire (twenty-four), of Wilson Street, Clitheroe, was too ill to go to her work as a packer at the bleach works her mother, Jane Ainscough Derbyshire, thought that she was suffering from influenza – or at least that is what she told the coroner at the inquest into her daughter's death in 1919. Although the doctors Mrs Derbyshire had called in to tend to her sick daughter operated on Alice on 14 June, Mrs Derbyshire would not allow her to go to hospital because she did not think she was well enough to be moved, and the girl died on the evening of 16 June. A post mortem showed that her death was due to septicaemia, resulting from peritonitis, which was due to a wound. Or, as the coroner put it to the jury, 'Boiled down, it simply means that an illegal operation was performed on her.'

Police called to the death scene found a rusty blowpipe and two pieces of wire in Alice's bedroom, which Mrs Derbyshire claimed belonged to a lodger who used them to repair watches and confirmed that she had put them in a drawer in her daughter's room as there was no space for them anywhere else in the house. She also told the inquest that she had no knowledge whatsoever of Alice having an abortion, nor had she known that her daughter had experienced a previous miscarriage in May 1918. Mrs Derbyshire described herself as being 'innocent as a lamb', and stated that she had only realised how ill her daughter had become when she began to lose a lot of blood.

Another main witness at the inquest was Walter Wallbank, a clean-shaven young man who worked at the cement works and lived in Cross Street. Wallbank admitted that he had been 'walking out' with Alice Derbyshire for several months, but had no idea that she was pregnant. He denied that her condition had anything to do with him and told the coroner that he had 'never said a wrong word to the girl'. The coroner sharply retorted, 'I don't say you said a wrong word, what I want to know is: have you ever been intimate with her?' To which Wallbank replied, 'No sir; never in my life.' The coroner then remarked how it was 'a funny state of affairs' for a man to walk out with a woman, and be ignorant of the fact that she was in a certain condition. Evidence was presented to show that Wallbank had been to Blackpool with Alice on several occasions, but Wallbank denied that they had been there to seek an abortion at any time.

A juror, Mr Tomlinson, then asked the medical witness if it was probable that the blowpipe and wire found at Wilson Street had been used in the abortion and if it was possible that such an operation could be self-performed. The witness answered both questions in the affirmative. Mr Tomlinson's stated opinion was, 'I don't think we have had the whole truth from either of these two witnesses' (Derbyshire and Wallbank). The coroner agreed that he was probably right about this and advised the jury to return an 'open verdict', which, he said, would practically amount to a verdict of 'murder against some person or persons unknown.' This would allow the police a free hand to prosecute a suspect if further evidence emerged and, according to a report in the *Clitheroe Times* of Friday 20 June 1919, this is what they did.

The same newspaper also carried a request to writers of certain anonymous letters to the police, received in relation to the case, to get in touch with the force in person and without delay.

A Celebration Gone Wrong (1933)

Susan Gudgeon, a thirty-six-year-old machinist, and Arthur Denham, aged forty and a bank cashier, had been friends for some considerable time and went out and about together, mostly to Clitheroe's pubs, about two or three times a week. On Friday 24 December 1933, the evening before Susan's birthday, they called into the Royal Oak hotel, Waterloo at about 8.15 p.m. They celebrated happily with an assortment of alcoholic drinks before leaving just over an hour later. Miss Gudgeon returned to the house in Back Commons, which she shared with her father, whilst Denham went to the Station Hotel to have his glass hip flask filled with a quarter pint of rum, which he took away.

The Royal Oak, Clitheroe.

The next anyone saw of the pair was when, later that night, Susan banged on the door of the doctor's surgery asking that he be told to come quickly to her house, as Mr Denham was 'very ill'. Despite the cold night air, she was wearing only a thin dress, appeared to be out of breath, and was agitated. When Dr Shortt received the message, he dashed off to Back Commons, where he met Susan and her father approaching the house. On entering the hallway, they found Arthur Denham lying on his back with a small wound in his chest. He was dead.

When Susan became aware of this, she flung herself down on the living-room hearth rug and sobbed bitterly. She told Dr Shortt that Denham had attacked her, so she had struck out in self-defence with the first thing she could grab, her father's knife. The doctor sent for the police, who cautioned Gudgeon before taking a statement from her. The statement, which was included in reports in the *Clitheroe Advertiser and Times* on 8 December 1933 and 26 January 1934, read thus:

> I, Susan Gudgeon, after having been cautioned by the chief constable that anything I say will be taken down and given in evidence, wish to make this voluntary statement.
>
> About 8 p.m. today, Friday, November 24th, 1933, Arthur Milnes Denham took me to the Royal Oak to celebrate my birthday, which is tomorrow, the 25th. He then went to the Station Hotel for some rum, and then came back here. When he came home he tried to abuse me. He called me all sorts of awful names. He struck me with his hands on my face. He tore my beads off. He knocked me with the shovel. He kicked the dog, which I was calling for my protection.
>
> He tried to take advantage of me, and I grabbed at my father's knife, which was on the mantelpiece. I hit him with it. He tried to get it off me, and hit me back. I threw it as we were struggling. I was struggling when I hit him.
>
> Arthur went towards the front door and he dropped. There was some rum in a glass. I took it to him and he gulped it back. I pulled his shirt back. I ran for Dr Shortt. He was not dead then.
>
> I picked the knife up with the intention of frightening him so that he would desist attacking me. He got me by the throat when I was stood by the fire, so I put up my hand and grabbed the knife. I have read this statement, and I have had it read over to me, and it is correct.

The Inn at Coldwell – now an outdoor centre.

Evidence, including the broken beads, and angry red wheals around Susan's neck, seemed to back up this version of events. The policemen who had attended the scene, Dr Shortt and the police surgeon, were unanimous in believing Susan but the magistrates sent her for trial at Lancaster Assizes, on a charge of murder.

On 25 January 1934, the trial judge, Mr Justice Rigby Swift, gave a very clear indication that the murder charge could not be proved and counsel for the Crown agreed that the charge be reduced to one of manslaughter. After a three-hour hearing, the jury acquitted Susan Gudgeon of all charges.

COLDWELL

Coldwell lies in the hills above Nelson, looking down on the valley from the opposite side to Pendle Hill, and stands on an ancient packhorse route between Colne and Halifax. The Inn at Coldwell was a coaching inn on this route and there was once a Templar cross on its south gable to show that it was a place of hospitality and refuge. Two large reservoirs now dominate the area and have become a haven for local wildlife.

Coldwell reservoir.

The natural amphitheatre where gamblers gathered.

The Coldwell Raid (1922)

The Coldwell Raid, designed to put an end to the notorious gambling school held regularly in a hollow on the moors above Nelson, was later likened by the press to a 'well-planned military manoeuvre'. This may seem a rather 'over the top' solution, but over 100 men were often present during these illegal sessions at Coldwell and almost seventy gamblers were prosecuted following the raid on 17 October 1922.

The local police had made many previous efforts to close down the operation. Wives complained that their husbands were squandering money they could ill afford there, and were selling their wives' and daughters' jewellery and the shirts off their own backs (literally) to raise stake money. The stakes were high and gambling on coins tossed from a wooden board took place almost every afternoon and evening, with Sunday being the busiest day. The men attending these sessions ranged from doctors, dentists and solicitors through to the many poor and unemployed locals who were seeking a quick remedy to their monetary problems. It was not uncommon to see respectable men, still carrying their bibles, making their way to Coldwell after attending Sunday services at church or chapel. Jewellery could be bought cheaply around the gaming area, with pies, cakes and other refreshments served at the ringside. This all added up to big business, and the enterprise was well run, with its own binocular-wielding lookouts and 'sergeants' to ensure security and sound the alarms if they spotted police approaching. This meant that by the time the police arrived, all signs of illegal activity had been hidden and all they found were groups of men chatting, walking and enjoying the countryside. Eventually, two unknown policemen from outside the area were brought in to infiltrate the gambling fraternity, and managed to gather sufficient evidence for their superior officers to plan the raid.

At about 3 p.m. on a dull October Sunday, the Nelson officers left their coach at the top of Barkerhouse Road, they climbed the wall and began to approach the natural moorland amphitheatre where the gamblers gathered. At the same time, a coach came along the top road from Trawden whilst yet another approached from Padiham via Briercliffe and Haggate. In this way, over 100 policemen, led by Superintendent Cleal and Chief Inspector Riley, completely encircled the ring.

By the time the sentries sounded the alarm, it was too late for the majority of the gamblers to escape – although many tried to make a bolt for it by scaling walls and climbing ditches. Whichever way they went, they found policemen blocking their paths, and most gave up quietly. Some feigned innocent reasons for their presence on the moors, one man even pretending to be absorbed in a copy of *The Count of Monte Cristo*, but all who were caught there that day were taken to Nelson police station in a convoy of charabancs (coaches).

The courts who tried the sixty-seven men involved imposed fines totalling almost £2,000 upon them, and Coldwell was finally rid of the 'moral blot' that was the gambling school.

COLNE

There have been settlements around Colne for many centuries. Bronze Age and Iron Age remains found nearby testify to this, as do the many Roman coins discovered in the area. The parish church dates back to the eleventh century, and Wallace Hartley, the bandmaster of the RMS *Titanic*, was born in Greenfield Lane. A monument to him stands in Albert Road.

A Murderous Rabble (1840)

In 1839, an act 'for the establishment of county and district constables' came into being and Pendle and the Ribble Valley received their compliment of top-hatted police constables. This new rural police force proved very unpopular, being seen as oppressive, expensive and brutal.

Statue of Wallace Hartley.

Soon, anti-police demonstrations organised by Chartists and other social agitators took place throughout the area in protest against the new regime.

In 1840, many special constables were sworn in to help the local police control and dispel these gatherings but rioting took place in Colne at Easter of that year when the troops had to be called out to regain order, and by August resentment and unrest were running rife in the streets. A public meeting at the grammar school, organised to discuss ways to appease the weavers, Chartists and anti-police factions, was soon taken over by the agitators, and the police, magistrates and other public figures had to retreat and reconvene at the King's Head Inn.

The unrest escalated over the next few days, gathering momentum and more participants, until by Monday 10 August the streets of Colne were swarming with a furious rabble. Fearing the likely consequences, the magistrates appointed around seventy special constables to help the twenty-six or so regular policemen to disperse the crowds. Each special constable was given a truncheon.

The old King's Head. (courtesy of Lancashire Library and Information Services)

Above: Clayton Street. (courtesy of Lancashire County Library and Information Services)

Left: Joseph Halstead's grave.

Opposite: Old Carry Hey farm, c. 1910. (courtesy of Lancashire Library and Information Services)

At about 9.30 p.m., a magistrate faced the mob to read the Riot Act, explaining to them that their remaining on the streets following this reading would constitute a felony. The magistrate repeated the reading of the act several more times around the town and the rabble seemed to disperse. The constables were then dispatched in small groups to check that the back streets were cleared of protesters, and that the threatened riot had ground to a halt.

One of these groups went into the back of Clayton Street, where a mob carrying lengths of iron railings set upon them, and a special constable, Joseph Halstead, was killed. He was battered about the head so badly that his face was barely recognisable beneath the cuts, bruises and swelling. A witness recognised the man who had wielded the fatal blows as weaver Richard Boothman, who was consequently brought to trial and convicted of killing Halstead, despite his long protestations of innocence.

Boothman's death sentence was eventually commuted to transportation for life, and he sailed to Tasmania aboard the *Barbarossa*, arriving in Hobart in January 1842. He died in Launceston, Tasmania in 1877, still hoping that his relatives would petition for his return home on the grounds that he had been wrongly convicted.

Joseph Halstead was buried in his mother's grave in Colne cemetery, where the headstone reads:

Here lieth all that is mortal of Martha, wife of John Halstead of Colne, who departed this life the 18th day of December 1829, aged 60 years.

Also of Joseph their son who was barbarously murdered in the 44th year of his age while engaged in his duty as a special constable during the riot which took place in this town on the evening of the 10th August 1840, leaving four orphan children to lament their loss.

The Stainsby Sex Crimes (1855)

In the summer of 1885 Robert Stainsby, a weaver of Lenches, Colne, appeared at Colne Police Court charged with sex offences involving two different women; the alleged offences had taken place on 22 July.

Old Carry Hey Farm *c*. 1910. (courtesy of Lancashire Library and Information services)

Mire Ridge.

The first charge related to the indecent assault of Mary Alice Laycock, a nineteen-year-old unmarried Colne woman, who was still feeling shaken and shocked by her ordeal. She testified that a few days earlier she had been walking with her nine-year-old sister on the road from Colne to Trawden: as they followed the footpath between High Carry Hey and Lower Carry Hey, a man came across the field and asked, 'Where are you going in such a hurry?' Miss Laycock had not replied, and the man had thrown his coat, which he had been carrying on his arm, over her head, pushed her to the ground and put his hand up her clothes. She had screamed all the while until the man eventually ran off in the direction of Colne. Miss Laycock then ran down to the farmhouse at Carry Hey and told the farmer's wife what had happened. Mary finished her testimony by saying that she did not know her attacker, and had never seen him before.

Ten-year-old Alfred Blackburn then gave his evidence: he recounted how he had seen the attack on Miss Laycock take place just as she had described, adding that he recognised her assailant as Robert Stainsby, who he knew quite well. The boy stated that the incident had been so frightening that he had turned in his tracks and run home.

Other witnesses swore they had seen Stainsby in the area at the time of the offence, but the accused insisted that it was a case of mistaken identity. He claimed that he had been at Mire Edge around noon, before spending the rest of the day relaxing in the grass at the edge of the woods before arriving home around half four in the afternoon. The bench then proceeded to hear the next, more serious case, against Stainsby.

Mary Ann Birtwistle, a tackler's wife from Trawden, told how on the same day that Mary Laycock was attacked she had also undergone a terrifying ordeal. She said that she had been on her way home from Colne market, where she had been shopping with her ten-year-old sister-in-law, Elizabeth Alice. It was about 4 p.m., and as they reached Mire Edge, a man came towards them down Cow Lane. As he approached them he said, 'I will learn you, you bloody devil', and roughly took hold of her by the shoulders.

Naturally, she had begun to scream, at which her attacker put one hand tightly over her mouth whilst hitting her with a flat blow to the face with the other. Mrs Birtwistle then indicated the black eye she still bore as a result of this violence. As she struggled to escape, the man threw her to the ground and threatened to kill her if she did not 'hold her noise'. At this point, a frightened Elizabeth Alice ran off screaming, and the man then very forcefully raped his victim.

When the rapist finally released her and made his getaway, Mary Ann stoically gathered up her purchases, which had been strewn around in the mêlée, and was then met by her uncle and Police Constable Marsden, who had been roused by her sister-in-law (who later confirmed Mary Ann's story up to the point at which she had run for help). Both young women identified the prisoner in the dock, Stainsby, as the assailant.

Police Constable Marsden gave evidence that he had gone to interview the suspect at home later the same evening and found him to be perspiring and 'very much excited'. Stainsby's face and hands were badly scratched. The constable took him to the police station and charged him with the rape of Mary Ann Birtwistle, to which he replied, 'I didn't do it'. However, Mrs Birtwistle later picked him out in an identity parade.

Robert Stainsby was committed for trial at the Liverpool Summer Assizes, where he was found guilty of both offences. The judge, Mr Justice Manisty, remarked that 'there could be no doubt in the mind of any human being that the prisoner was guilty of the offences' and sentenced him to ten years of penal servitude.

An Ultimate Decision (1862)

Betty Moore, a thirty-two-year-old woman from the Keighley area, left her husband at the beginning of 1862 to become housekeeper to her uncle, Jacob Wood, and his son, William, at the Hare and Hounds public house at Black Lane Ends. Betty's relationship with her husband, Walker Moore, had been a stormy one and it was not the first time that the couple had separated.

On 4 April of the same year, Walker Moore and a friend, Joseph Metcalfe, decided to go to a foot race in Burnley, and Moore told Metcalfe that he must first call at the Hare and Hounds to get some money from his wife. When the men arrived at the pub, Betty refused to give any money to her husband and also turned down his request that she return home with him. A further plea that Betty sleep with him at the pub that night also received a negative reply and Walker Moore was allocated a bed in a shared room with Metcalfe and a potboy whom he quizzed about his wife's usual sleeping arrangements at the establishment. The boy told him that Betty sometimes slept in the room with him, whilst at other times she slept with her cousin William.

Early the following morning, Joseph Metcalfe went downstairs to find Walker already drinking both ale and spirits. Betty was in the same room, cleaning the fire irons. He then saw, as he testified at the trial at Lancaster Summer Assizes, Moore rise from his seat, take hold of his wife's head with his left hand and draw a blade across her throat with his right. Betty got to her feet, clutching her apron to her bleeding throat, at which point William Wood entered the room, caught her and laid her on a long settee, where she later died.

When Police Constable Charles Lord arrived at the scene and charged Moore with the murder of his wife, the accused man replied, 'I came on purpose to do it'. He went on to confirm that he had brought the razor with him expressly for that purpose. He then added that he would have been happier if he had cut William Wood's throat as well.

Black Lane Ends – formerly the Hare and Hounds.

The presiding Assizes judge at Moore's trial, Mr Baron Wilde, berated the prisoner in his closing remarks, saying that jealousy, unfounded or not, gave no immunity from the consequences of murder. Then, donning his black cap, he pronounced him guilty of his wife's murder and sentenced him to be hanged.

Moore retorted, 'Thank you, my lord, I wish you would take into consideration how you would feel if you had another man in bed with your wife.' Adding, as he was taken downstairs, 'I hope it will be your case.'

It is not recorded whether this malicious wish came to pass, but another one of Moore's predictions, that there was 'no rope in existence' that would hang him, certainly proved to be the truth.

On the morning of his hanging, Moore asked to visit the toilet during his exercise time. His guards allowed this, only to find their prisoner drowned in a large cistern of water in the lavatory block. Walker Moore had denied the hangman his job, and the gathered crowd their entertainment.

Shuffling the Cards (1905)

When the police at Colne received several complaints that an elderly woman was telling fortunes by means of a pack of cards, they enlisted their wives to help with their investigation – and when elderly Margaret Whalley was prosecuted for the offence, they were the chief prosecution witnesses.

Rosaline Bell, whose husband was stationed at Foulridge, told the court that she had visited Mrs Whalley's home with Emily Horsfall, wife of a PC from Colne. She said that the defendant

Houses near to Margaret Whalley's home. (courtesy of Lancashire Library and Information Services)

had welcomed them into her home, where there was a pack of cards on the table. After looking at her left hand, Whalley told her she was a jealous person and asked her to shuffle the cards: Whalley then told her that a sudden death was coming, as was a letter, and that a fair-haired woman was her enemy. She also informed her that she would marry within three months and move 'across the water', where she would go into a business which would make her a lot of money. The cards were shuffled again and Whalley declared that 'death' turned up at every turn of the cards. Mrs Bell handed over a shilling for the privilege of receiving this insight into her future life before Emily Horsfall took her place at the table. Mrs Horsfall told a similar story of shuffling the cards, saying that Whalley had informed her she would marry twice. She had also given the old woman a shilling.

Constable Horsfall related how he and PC Kirkwood had approached the house as the women were leaving and Mrs Whalley had told them that they were her nieces from Keighley. When Constable Horsfall challenged her about the alleged offence she replied, 'You will have to prove it first', adding that she could not tell her own future, never mind anybody else's.

Sadly, this proved to be the case, as the old fortune-teller did not foresee that she would be found guilty and fined twenty shillings with costs.

Killed by her Sister-in-Law (1933)

In 1933, two sisters shared a home in Selby Street, Colne. One sister, Mrs Whittaker, took care of the other, Miss Mary Hodgson, who suffered from a crippling arthritic condition. Their sister-in-law, Mrs Fanny Hodgson, the widow of a prominent local manufacturer, was a regular visitor to Selby Street and the women appeared to be 'on very affectionate terms.'

In May 1933, another such visit took place, but on the following day, Mrs Whittaker found Miss Mary dead in her bedroom: the room was in such a state that it was obvious that there had been a violent struggle, and she quickly summoned the police. When the police surgeon examined the body, he found a handkerchief had been stuffed tightly in the dead woman's throat, along with her upper dentures, thus resulting in asphyxiation.

After talking to the distraught Mrs Whittaker, the police arrested Fanny Hodgson at her home in Charles Street, Nelson, and she was committed for trial on a charge of murder. However, at Liverpool Assizes on 11 June 1933, the deputy medical officer of Strangeways Prison told the court that it was his opinion that the prisoner was not of sound mind, whereupon the judge, Mr Justice McNaughton, instructed the jury to find Mrs Hodgson unfit to plead. This they did; they further ordered that she 'be detained during his Majesty's pleasure.'

Fanny Hodgson was sent to Broadmoor Criminal Lunatic Asylum in Berkshire, where she died from cancer the following year.

COURT LEET

In the Middle Ages, the lord of the manor held police jurisdiction under the 'frankpledge system'. The custom of the court baron exercising these powers became known as the Court Leet. This was an annual court of record, which depended upon royal franchise for its jurisdiction and had the task of presenting crimes and pleas to a jury. Constables were appointed at the court, as were other officials such as aletesters (responsible for weight, measure and quality of this important beverage), surveyors of hedges and ditches, and pinders. The steward of the court acted as judge, whilst the bailiff ran the system and made sure that fines and penalties were levied correctly. Later, the Court Leet became the lowest court of criminal jurisdiction, dealing with offences considered too minor to be go before the Quarter Sessions or Assizes.

Selby Street.

Downham village stream.

These are extracts from Clitheroe Court Leet records, which I found at Clitheroe library:

20 April 1621 – The jury presented the town of Pendleton for not hanging a gate between the Higher Moor and their lane at Pendleton Mill.

18 April 1678 – Roger Kitching and Alexander Hall were presented for not repairing a footbridge called Standen Bridge, leading between Clitheroe and Whalley, to the great danger of his majesty's subjects. They were amerced 12 shillings and the jury ordered them to repair the same before the 24 June, under the penalty of £5.

7 May 1691 – Richard Slater was presented for 'leading the stones out of the brook leading to Pendleton Mill being annoyance to their majesties and all their liege people'. The jury laid a pain of £4, 'that he cause the way to be made sufficient'.

DOWNHAM

The village of Downham lies tucked into a fold at the bottom of Pendle Hill. It has changed little over centuries and has had a strong connection to the Assheton family since medieval times.

It was a haunt of the infamous, if misrepresented, Pendle witches, and is the place where the film *Whistle down the Wind* was filmed in the early 1960s, when several of the villagers were given roles alongside Hayley Mills.

Catastrophic Disaster (1945)

When it looked like a sudden snowfall might prevent the Hon. Mrs Sylvia Assheton of Red Syke, Twiston, from attending a morning meeting with the bailiff of the estate she managed, she tried to ring him several times, but there was no reply. Thinking that his phone must be out of order, she risked the drive to West Lane Farm, Downham, the home of Bailiff Edward Cornell, his wife and three young children.

Mrs Assheton had been with Cornell and a number of other farmers at a meeting the previous evening and all had seemed well with him, but when she arrived at the farm, she met farm worker Albert Hartley, who was beginning to become concerned about the Cornells. He had noticed the lights were still on in the family's bedrooms, but the doors were locked and he could not get in, or get a reply to his knocking. Mrs Assheton sent for the estate joiner, who forced open a window through which they climbed.

In the kitchen, the previous evening's supper pots were still on the table, and none of the family was in evidence either there or in the living room. Calling as they went, Mrs Assheton and her companions went upstairs, fearing something was very wrong, and entered the first bedroom: there they found Cornell on the bed, lying on his right elbow, his nightclothes covered in blood. His wife was next to him, also drenched in blood, with her arms and head lolling lifelessly over the edge of the bed. On the covers between them was a humane killer that the estate manager had bought in 1940 in case any livestock were struck by enemy fire and needed putting down. The weapon, which was always kept in the farm office, was pointing towards Cornell.

As they stood there horrified, Cornell moved slightly and one eye flickered open. Mrs Assheton ran downstairs to telephone the police and ambulance. She then dashed back to check on the children and found even more mayhem in their bedroom: the two girls, Sylvia (six) and Dorothy Hazel (eighteen months) were quite obviously dead from head wounds, whilst their brother Edward (five) was just barely alive. She carried the little boy downstairs and made him comfortable in an armchair until the emergency services arrived. The ambulance took father and son to Blackburn Infirmary where they both later died without regaining consciousness.

Meanwhile, the police detectives called to the farmhouse made a thorough search. They noted that the heavy humane killer was uncocked, and that it was covered in so much blood that taking fingerprints from it proved impossible. There were ten spent cartridges scattered about the upper floor and ten wounds on the bodies. They also noticed several large bloody footprints leading from the children's room to Mr and Mrs Cornell's bed.

Neighbours, friends and fellow farm-workers were shocked by the incident, which the press termed 'a catastrophic disaster', and insisted that the Cornells had been a loving happy family with no obvious problems. They considered Mrs Cornell to be a good wife to her husband, who had a reputation as a hard worker and a fair man.

After hearing at the ensuing inquest that Cornell's head wound was probably self-inflicted, the coroner advised the jury that they must decide whether he had been of sound mind or, as he colloquially put it, 'crackers' at the time of the murders. He emphasised that the time it would have taken the man to kill all his family with all the 'padding around between rooms' that occurred would seem to indicate that this had not been the act of a 'maniacal murderer.'

After a brief retirement, the jury's verdict was that Edward Cornell committed *Felo de se* (self murder) after murdering his wife and children.

West Lane – the farm has been demolished.

EARBY

Earby appears in the Domesday Book named as 'Eurebi in the Manor of Thornton'. Once known as a lead-mining community, it now has several light-engineering premises dotted between its older cottages and rows of terraced houses.

'I'll Swing Like a Man' (1892)

Moses Cudworth and his wife, Eliza, lived in Wesley Street in the ominously named Earby district known locally as 'Whitechapel', as was the London area where Jack the Ripper had slashed and murdered just a few years previously. They were both weavers in their forties, worked together at Albion Mill and had four children ranging from four to eighteen years old. Their marriage had deteriorated with time, largely due to Moses' heavy drinking and jealousy towards his wife. He had become increasingly violent towards Eliza and as his behaviour grew more erratic, he began to insist that she accompany him everywhere he went, including the pubs where he did his drinking. Eliza also reached a point where she was drinking too much because of this and the couple's rowdy behaviour and drunken public arguments became commonplace.

The Cudworths sometimes took in lodgers to help ends meet, and one of these was a young man who took a strong liking to Eliza. Moses became convinced that the two were having an affair, citing such ordinary occurrences as their cups being placed close together on the table as a sure sign of their infidelity. When Moses cracked and threw the young man out of his house, his behaviour became even more irrational and unpredictable. Eliza told her sister-in-law,

Ellen Fylon, that she had recently found a large clasp-knife under her husband's pillow, and when she asked him about it he had answered, 'Oh, I've been cutting a bit of baccy (tobacco), and forgotten it.' Ellen felt uneasy about this, knowing that Eliza would not have mentioned the incident if she too had not felt concerned.

On Saturday 4 June, Moses and Eliza left Albion Mill together after a morning shift that ended at 12.30: it was the start of the Whitsuntide holiday and they decided they would go to the clogger's shop that afternoon to buy their youngest daughter, Kate, a pair of clogs. They had a couple of draughts of beer each before leaving, with Kate, to carry out their errand. Ellen Fylon (who lodged with the Cudworths along with her husband) saw them leave, but in a short while, Moses returned and asked her where Eliza was. Ellen replied that she thought they had gone to the clogger's together, at which Moses left. However, soon afterwards he returned to ask the same question (receiving a similar answer).

Half an hour later Ellen Fylon was called to a neighbour's house, where she found Moses with Kate sitting on his knee; he had blood on his hand and Ellen was now the one to ask where Eliza was. Moses said that Ellen would find her if she went to look, and pointing to his bloodied hand told her it was Eliza's blood. At this news, Ellen ran down the street and as she approached Muck Lane, she met a Mr Metcalfe who told her that a woman's body had been found in the Old Barnoldswick Lane. They met PC White and went with him to the scene where they saw that the dead woman was Eliza. Her head and face had been brutally battered and in her left hand she still clutched a clump of hair that was the same colour as Moses' whiskers.

Meanwhile, Moses remained at the neighbour's house, drinking beer and describing how he had killed his wife after an argument in which a knife had been drawn before he had 'punched her in th'yed [the head].' When PC White went there to arrest him, Moses objected to the use of handcuffs saying, 'What are you putting them on for? I've done the deed; I've killed her; I shall never repent it; I'll swing like a man.'

On the following Wednesday afternoon, a large number of people attended Eliza Cudworth's funeral, which was paid for by a village collection (as were the mourning clothes worn by the Cudworth children).

Moses Cudworth was taken by train to Skipton, as Earby had no lock-up. He struggled on the way to the station, hanging on to garden railings and lashing out at his escort, so they tied his legs together and forced him into a local milkman's cart, completing their journey followed by a motley crowd shouting and jeering at the prisoner all the way.

The following Monday, Cudworth appeared at Skipton Magistrate's Court where he was charged with the murder of Eliza Cudworth in Old Lane, Hill Top, Earby, and remanded in custody until his case was heard at West Riding Assizes (held in Leeds Town Hall). He pleaded 'not guilty', but after hearing all the evidence the jury did not take long to reach a verdict of 'guilty of wilful murder', whereupon the presiding judge (Mr Justice Grantham) donned his black cap to pronounce the death sentence upon him.

On Thursday 18 August, Moses Cudworth walked from his cell to the yard at Armley prison. As he climbed the fifteen steps to the scaffold, the prison bell tolled to announce that he was about to 'swing like a man'.

ECCLESIASTICAL COURTS

A register of the Ecclesiastical Court of Whalley Abbey from between 1515 and 1538 refers to an ecclesiastical court in the area principally taking place at Whalley church. For most of this time, the judge of the court was Christopher Smith, the prior, who lies buried within the church.

The cases presented to the Ecclesiastical Court were very varied, ranging from accusations of slander and matrimonial disputes to non-attendance at church services. Even minor misdemeanours, such as talking in church or breach of promise, were dealt with, and punishments thought appropriate for the deed meted out. One punishment was to make the offenders walk barefoot either in the church or around the grounds, whilst holding a lighted candle in supplication. The most severe sentence given was that of excommunication, which struck terror into the God-fearing parishioners. The register also records that a group of offenders from Pendle were forced to carry heavy stones to the church in Downham, as penance for 'profanation of holidays', whilst one Gilbert Marsden is mentioned for having brought a suit against his wife, whom he alleged was so violent that he 'dare not live with her'.

An ecclesiastical court sometimes convened at St Michael's chapel in Clitheroe Castle. The register records that at one court session there Margaret Crossley was charged with 'being a notorious swearer'; Elizabeth Medwood with 'absenting herself from church'; and the wife of Nicholas Shaw with 'washing clothes on a Saturday evening'.

FENCE

Situated at the western end of Pendle Hill, Fence takes its name from the enclosures there that once existed to hold stags in the days when the forest of Pendle was a plentiful hunting ground.

Cuckstool Lane
Cuckstool Lane, leading from the Padiham bypass down to Brierfield, got its name in the days when it was a dirt road from Wheatley Lane through New Laund. At one point, it passed close to a part of the river that was deep enough to allow a cucking stool, or ducking stool, to be immersed.

According to Wikipedia, the term cucking stool literally means 'defecation chair', from the early practice of using commodes for the punishment. Sometimes they were just chairs in which the victims, mainly but not exclusively women, would be tied and exposed outside her home for public humiliation, but they appear to have gradually morphed into ducking stools, providing better entertainment for the raucous crowds that would attend such punishments.

In medieval times and beyond, women who were convicted of public order offences such as brawling, drunkenness and prostitution were often sentenced to punishment by this method. The prisoners were strapped into a purpose-built chair, swung out over the river (or deep pond) and ducked into the water a number of times, depending on the severity of their crime. During this soaking, the offender would also be subject to ribald comments (and worse) flung at her as she sat immobilised. The practice appears to have died out during the middle of the eighteenth century.

GISBURN

The village of Gisburn lies on the road between Clitheroe and Skipton alongside the river Ribble and surrounded by farmland and forest. Lord Ribblesdale's family home was once at Gisburn Park (now a private hospital) and a medieval church dominates the centre of the still partly cobbled village.

Clitheroe Castle.

Cuckstool Lane.

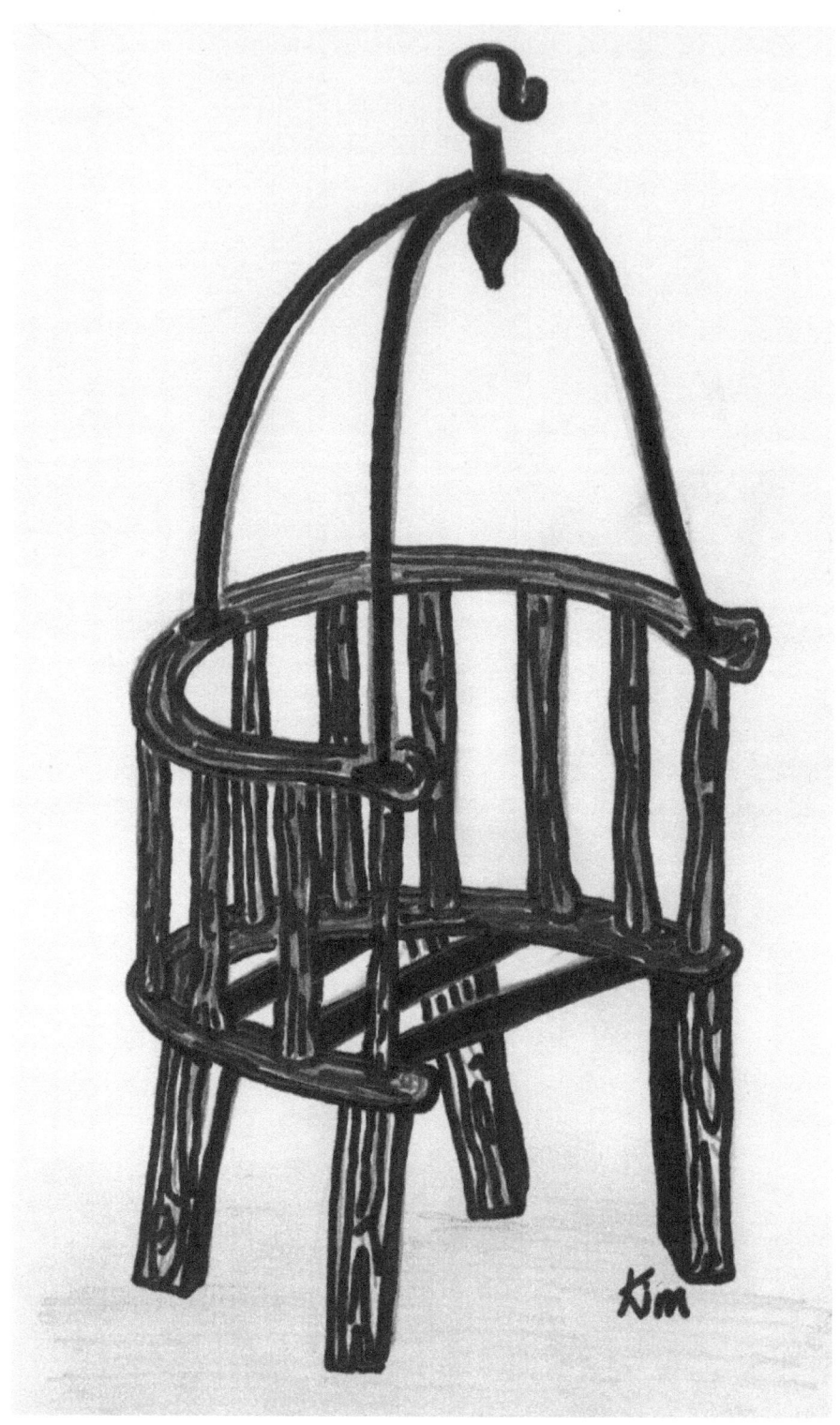

Ducking stool.

Cock Fighting (1855)

It was 'standing room only' at Bolton-by-Bowland Petty Sessions, when twenty-three men faced the court accused of being involved with a cock fight held at Nappa on the 10 March 1855. Because of the large number of defendants on trial, two of their solicitors wanted their clients to be identified and tried separately, but the magistrates would not deviate from the normal procedure and insisted that the men each stand up as their name was called, in order to be identified and make their plea.

Mr Foreshaw of Preston prosecuted on behalf of the Royal Society for the Prevention of Cruelty to Animals, and described how the accused had arrived by train to hold the fight, a crime under the second section of the Cruelty to Animals Act. He said the men had assembled at the secluded spot near to Nappa Farm carrying all the appliances and paraphernalia of cock fighting. They had brought several birds, trimmed and spurred with steel spurs about two inches long, and set them at each other for their barbarous 'sport'.

One defence solicitor, Mr Backhouse, asked the Bench if they would accept a plea of guilty from his clients in exchange for a fine, or other non-custodial sentence, as otherwise they would plead 'not guilty' and the case would prove to be a very lengthy one. The magistrates replied that they were not prepared to enter into any bargaining, but that Mr Backhouse 'had better trust to the common sense of the magistrates'. All the men, save one, then entered a guilty plea and were fined ten shillings with costs (about two pounds each in total), or a month's imprisonment.

The exception was George Tillotson, a signalman at Newsholme railway station. His solicitor claimed that he 'could not plead guilty even if the case lasted all day'. He told the magistrates that Tillotson, a complete stranger to the rest of the defendants, was off-duty and visiting his brother at Nappa Farm on the day in question. He happened to see a crowd gathering in a nearby field and went to see what was happening. He had no idea beforehand that it was a cock fight, and was apprehended as he made to leave in disgust at the spectacle. After hearing this statement, Mr Foreshaw withdrew the summons against Tillotson.

HALMOTE COURTS

Under feudal law, the Halmote, or Manor, Courts dealt with matters pertaining to tenants of the lord of the manor. It had criminal and civil jurisdiction and was often the place where the lord of the manor's representatives would come to collect the tenant farmers' rent. The name derives from the Saxon 'Hallmoot', meaning a 'meeting in the hall'.

The seventeenth-century Moot Court at Clitheroe was held in part of the building that now houses the library. The dungeons where unfortunate prisoners were kept were hewn out of the solid rock face beneath the edifice, and even now tend to flood in severe weather.

For centuries, the court for Burnley and the forest of Pendle was held at Ightenhill, with its officials travelling to convene the court in areas such as Clitheroe, Colne and Accrington. About 1520, the forest of Pendle separated from this judicial circuit and held the area's Halmote Court at Higham Hall. A steward presided over proceedings with a jury made up from tenants of the many Pendleside 'booths', or hamlets. Tenants were fined for non-attendance and the decisions reached by the court had to be obeyed.

Fines were meted out for such misdemeanours as diverting streams, allowing animals to graze on other people's land and harbouring illicit card games and other types of gambling. It ensured that roads were kept passable and in good repair and imposed fines on those who had their corn ground elsewhere than at the King's Mill. As late as 1564, there is a record of one John Robinson of Old Laund Booth being fined for keeping an unlawful hand mill.

Dungeons under old Moot Court building (now the library).

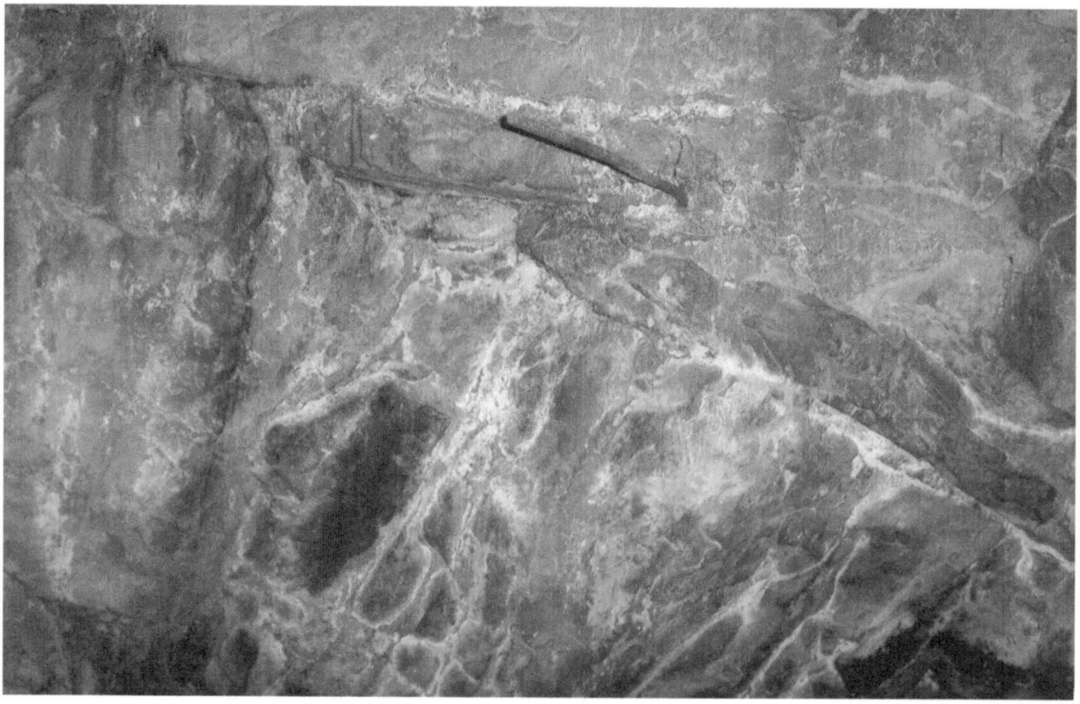

Cell walls hewn from the rock face.

Higham Hall – once used as a Halmote Court.

HURST GREEN

Hurst green lies close to the river Hodder, between Longridge and Clitheroe. The village has strong links with the Jesuit College at Stoneyhurst Hall, built in 1592 by Richard Shireburn, and is at the heart of the countryside thought to have been the inspiration for Tolkien's 'Middle Earth'.

Stand and Deliver!
In the seventeenth and eighteenth centuries, it was quite common for highwaymen to stop stagecoaches and horse riders as they travelled along public highways. These robbers, usually on horseback, would draw their pistols and threaten the travellers with violence if they refused to hand over their money and valuables.

One such highwayman was Ned King who, dressed in red coat, frilled white shirt and fashionable breeches, regularly accosted his victims on the lanes around Hurst Green, Dutton, and Clitheroe. King knew the times that stagecoaches were due to take a rest stop at the Punchbowl Inn and it was rumoured that he was in league with the landlord, who would inform him of any wealthy customers. When the king's troops were ordered to rid the area of its scourge of highwaymen and footpads, they went to the Punchbowl looking for Ned King, knowing it was his favourite watering hole. Ned hid in the inn's hay barn and shot four soldiers before receiving several shots to his body and being overpowered. The troops chained the highwayman and pulled him behind a horse to the old gibbet at the top of nearby Gallows Lane. They hanged him and left his body to hang for several weeks as a warning to others contemplating a similar career.

Stoneyhurst College.

Sign at the Punchbowl Inn, depicting Ned King.

Cottages at Hurst Green.

Murderous Mary (1835)

On Monday 17 March 1835, Mary Holden, a twenty-seven-year-old woman from Hurst Green, stood trial at Lancaster Assizes accused of the wilful murder of her husband, Rodger, in February 1834. Newspaper reports of the trial describe her as 'a decent looking woman' who appeared indifferent to the proceedings, and stated that she 'never shed a tear' during the duration of her ordeal.

Rodger Holden had been a weaver and had been married to Mary for about six years prior to his death. Their union had produced two children, one of whom died at a young age, and according to several witnesses, their relationship had gradually deteriorated to the point where they had become 'on very bad terms' during their last two years together.

One witness, William Chippendale, told the court that he had been at the couple's house three or four weeks before Rodger's sudden demise, and had been present when a bitter and heated argument that had taken place between the pair. During the row Rodger had called his wife 'a damned bad one', to which Mary had replied, 'as bad as I have been I shall be a great deal worse yet', adding that she would 'play him such a trick as he was little aware of.'

Another witness, Edmund Tomlinson, a local shopkeeper, was called to testify how Mary had called in at his shop on 17 or 18 February 1834 and asked him for six pennyworth of flea powder. Tomlinson told Mrs Holden that he had none in stock, but his servant, Harry Bradley, would get some for her when he next went into the nearest town of Blackburn. Harry Bradley confirmed this, as did the Blackburn druggist, Alexander Maxwell, who told the court how he had sold Bradley half-a-pound of arsenic wrapped in two folds of paper which he labelled 'ARSENIC – POISON.' Edmund Tomlinson said that he had later sold the arsenic to Mary Holden.

A neighbour of the Holdens, James Parker, then testified that he had met Rodger in William Chippendale's barn on the evening of 26 February and had found his friend so ill that he felt obliged to carry him home. Rodger had told him that he felt as though he had been 'nettled in his bowels' and was unable to walk. On arriving home Rodger had accused his wife of poisoning him, but Mary denied it, saying that he was always falsely accusing her of some misdeed or another. Parker then told how Rodger had asked him to examine the teapot, which proved, unusually for the practice of the time, to have been freshly washed out. He noticed some white powder in the spout that he tested and found to taste of lime. Mary had then harangued him, saying, 'dost thou think I have poisoned the fellow?', to which he made no reply, and having helped her to put the sick man to bed, he took the teapot home with him, and later passed it to Chippendale for safekeeping. Parker continued his testimony by telling how he had returned to the Holdens' home and given his friend some sweet oil in milk to alleviate his suffering, but Rodger Holden had died about 10.30 p.m. the same evening.

In his earlier testimony, William Chippendale had also described receiving the teapot from Parker, and had told how he had gone to see Mary the day after her husband's death and asked her if she had put poison into the pot. She had replied 'yes,' but added, 'I may have saved my own life through it, for I neither gave it to him, nor told him to take it.'

Mary confirmed this when called to speak in her own defence, claiming that it was her intention to mix the poison with the dregs of tea left in the pot, so that she could sprinkle the mixture about the house to rid it of fleas. She insisted that she had not given her husband poison or told him to drink from the pot, although she had put the powder in there in the hope that he would. She admitted throwing the rest of the arsenic into the nearby brook, and burning the paper in which it had been wrapped, after her husband's death.

The inquest report showed traces of arsenic in the victim's nostrils and throat, and stated that his stomach and intestines were badly inflamed as would be the case with arsenic poisoning. The judge directed the jury to take care they were satisfied of the prisoner's guilt before reaching a verdict but, apparently unconvinced by Mary's strange excuses and attempts to convince them of her innocence, they found her guilty of wilful murder.

The judge donned his black cap and after berating the prisoner on her evil ways and advising her to make her peace with God, passed sentence of death on Mary and decreed that she should be 'hung on Wednesday morning and buried within the precincts of Lancaster Prison'. According to the newspaper report, 'the prisoner then walked slowly from the bar, without manifesting any violent emotions, though it was evident that she suffered intensely.' Mary Holden was the last woman to be hanged at Lancaster Castle.

LANCASTER CASTLE

There were fortifications at the site of Lancaster Castle before Roman times and the keep of the castle, now a category 'C' prison, dates to the middle of the twelfth century. The bulk of the impressive edifice consists of later additions and was consistently maintained and improved because of its strategic importance.

Most convicted prisoners from Pendle and the Ribble Valley served their sentences at the castle until 1839, when the New Bailey prison was opened at Salford and felons sentenced to less than six months imprisonment were kept there. Long-term prisoners continued to be housed at Lancaster, where the condemned were publicly hanged at Gallows Hill. After 1800, they were openly dispatched within the prison walls at 'Hanging Corner' until 1863, when a

Lancaster Castle.

Inside the walls of Lancaster Castle.

new law required that executions should take place away from the public eye. The last hanging to take place at the prison was that of Thomas Rawcliffe, who was executed for the murder of his wife in 1911.

Until 1836, after which murder and attempted murder became the only crimes to attract the death penalty, those found guilty of far lesser crimes faced the death sentence. The following extracts from mid-eighteenth century records illustrate this:

August 1741: James Hanson – Horse theft
March 1756: Joseph Woolstencroft – Sent threatening letter
March 1765: Thomas Wilkinson – Highway robbery
August 1777: John Rotchley - Rape

Colne man Christopher Hartley was executed at Lancaster in August 1789, for the murder of Hannah Corbridge, and the Pendle Witches met a similar fate in 1612. Altogether, there were 200 people executed at Lancaster Castle, of which forty-three were hanged for murder – many of whom were dispatched by the same hangman, 'Old Ned' Barlow.

A Poisoner at Large (1910/1911)

Dark deeds were not always confined to the prisoners of Lancaster Castle, as the family of the custodian, William Hodgson Bingham, were to learn during the winter of 1910/1911.

Seventy-three-year-old Bingham had been in the post for over thirty years when his daughter, Annie, died on 12 November 1910. The cause of her death was given as 'hysteria and cerebral congestion'. Although touched by grief at his loss, William was relatively sprightly for his years, so it was another shock when he followed his daughter to the grave in January 1911. He had suffered severe vomiting and diarrhoea for three days before his death – the cause of which was certified as 'gastroenteritis'. Following this tragic turn of events, William's son, John Henry, assumed the mantle of custodian of the castle, where he was joined by his stepsister, Margaret, who took on the role of housekeeper for him. However, this arrangement did not last for long as within a few days Margaret developed similar symptoms to those that her father had suffered, and died. For some reason, despite the likeness in symptoms, her death was put down to a brain tumour.

James then turned to his sister, Edith Agnes, to take over housekeeping duties for him. Edith had been a trouble to the family for most of her twenty-nine years. She was educationally backwards, quarrelsome, and disposed to spending her time out and about with her boyfriend rather than in running the household. James, however, felt he had no alternative at the time, but by 11 August, he had had enough of her slovenly ways and sacked her, agreeing she could continue to lodge with him. He hired a new housekeeper from outside, but before she could take up the post, James suffered the same vomiting and diarrhoea and succumbed, as had his father and stepsister: this time, the coroner recorded 'arsenic poisoning' as the cause of death, and investigations began.

Less than an hour before collapsing whilst conducting a guided tour of the castle, James had eaten some beefsteak prepared by Edith, and when tins of 'acme weed killer' containing arsenic were found in a kitchen cupboard, she became the prime suspect. The police theorised that she had murdered James in a fit of pique at being sacked, but when the bodies of William and Margaret were exhumed, they too proved to contain large amounts of the poison. Annie, the first to die, had not ingested toxic material. It seemed that the deaths of James, Margaret and William were linked and after another brother, William Edward, gave a damning character reference for Edith, she faced trial at the Castle Assizes on 27 October 1911, charged with murdering all three.

The evidence against Edith was largely circumstantial, and witnesses testified to how distressed she had been at each family death. The maid who saw the accused woman cooking James' beefsteak saw nothing suspicious, and the defence lawyers argued that Edith was mentally incapable of carrying out such a careful plan. The jury agreed, and after retiring for less than half an hour, they declared her 'not guilty' on all charges. No one else was ever brought to justice for the murders and no further members of the Bingham family suffered a similar fate.

LANESHAWBRIDGE

Laneshawbridge is a settlement on the edge of Colne that developed around the place where old turnpike roads met and formed a crossroads. One road, an old herders' track dating back to the eighth century, leads to the Brontë town of Haworth.

A Very Unsavoury Case (1934)

Ada Ellen Rigg, a married woman who had separated from her husband, described herself as 'housekeeper' to Arthur Clegg, a gardener and porter at Hartley Hospital, Colne. However, it seems to have been generally acknowledged that the two lived together as man and wife at Flass Cottages, Laneshawbridge.

On the afternoon of 9 May 1934, the couple took a bus to visit Mrs Rigg's sister in Embsay, and then called at a public house in Skipton for a few drinks. On returning to Colne they drank in two more pubs before arriving at the Emmott Arms in Laneshawbridge at about 9.30 p.m. There the couple met up with a farmer friend, John Willie Dawson, and he joined them for more drinks and some supper. Clegg was buying. The three revellers left the Emmott Arms at about 10.30 p.m., intending to walk home along Emmott Lane together. All were affected by the amount of drink they had imbibed, Mrs Rigg and Mr Clegg especially so.

At about 12.30 a.m. on 10 May, the Broughton family at Ivy Cottage, Emmott Lane were disturbed by a ruckus outside. George, a leather worker, heard a man shout, 'I will put you in the ***** brook', to which another voice replied with a curse. He could not see who was shouting and, deciding it was just another drunken brawl, went back to bed. His father, Albert Broughton, awoke at about 3 a.m. to find his wife looking out of the window. He joined her but they could see nothing in the pitch blackness – but the screaming, shouting and cursing continued for quite a while.

When daylight came, Albert looked through the window again and saw Clegg, covered in blood and dirt, sitting on the grass verge mumbling to himself. Clegg then crossed the road where he seemed to be kicking something on the ground and Albert watched as he bent down and dragged someone out of the ditch by the ankles. Albert went to get help, and on returning with the constable, they found Mrs Rigg lying by the road. She was soaking wet, badly bruised about the face and semi-conscious. Her clothing was in disarray with her coat, hat, handbag and false teeth being in the stream, as were Clegg's hat and false teeth. The constable noted that Clegg, who was wandering around in a daze, appeared to be still under the influence of alcohol.

Mrs Rigg was admitted to Hartley Hospital where she was treated for her injuries and for exposure. When she recovered, she claimed that she could remember almost nothing about the night of the incident apart from feeling dizzy and falling down as she had walked up Emmott Lane. She could remember Clegg punching her as he tried to drag her to her feet, but could not recall if Dawson had been present at the time.

Laneshawbridge, showing the Emmott Arms at the top. (courtesy of Lancashire Library and Information Services)

Flass Cottages, attached to the old workhouse. (courtesy of Pat and Andrew Catlow)

Flass Cottages today – once a workhouse for the old and infirm.

John Willie Dawson claimed that they had left the pub together and Mrs Rigg fell down as they reached Ivy Cottage; for some reason, Clegg had then turned nasty towards him, swearing and grabbing him by the throat. He had retaliated by pushing Clegg away before leaving them to it and going home to bed. Clegg's version of events was somewhat different. He claimed that Dawson and Mrs Rigg had set off in front of him and when he caught up with them near to Ivy Cottage, they were 'on the job'. He shouted and swore at them both at which Dawson had attacked him. He had nothing to say about who had kicked Mrs Rigg.

Clegg faced the bench at Colne Police Court, where after hearing all the evidence the chairman, Mr J.L. Wildman, fined him ten shillings with costs, as it was his first offence and he was a very good worker. Mr Wildman declared that, 'The bench look upon this as a very unsavoury case, and it shows the evils of unrestricted drinking.'

He also berated John Willie Dawson for his part in the fiasco, pointing out that Mrs Rigg would not have been so ill if he had helped her home after her fall, and remarked that Clegg's own injuries seemed too severe to have been done by a drunken woman. Ada Ellen Rigg left her position as 'housekeeper' at Flass Cottages and moved to Brierfield.

LEAGRAM

Leagram is a small settlement lying seven miles to the north-west of Clitheroe. In the nineteenth century, it was considered a township in the parish of Whalley.

Grouse Poaching (1881)

In the nineteenth century, landowners were very protective of their shooting rights and were quick to prosecute anyone caught taking their birds or game. Mr Weld, of Leagram Hall, was no exception and employed a gamekeeper, John Dewhurst, to keep poachers off his estate.

In August 1881, Mr Dewhurst was on Saddle Side Fell with two companions when he heard shots and saw Charles and George Walmsley, local labourers, coming across the fell. Dewhurst and another gamekeeper followed the brothers and watched as they took it in turns to fire at the grouse, although they could not see whether the poachers had bagged their targets because of their covert positions. They counted seventeen shots before the Walmsleys made to leave the fell. When Dewhurst approached them, he took a gun from George whilst Charles made off across the countryside before he could apprehend him. The gamekeeper confronted him later in the day, and Charles denied having been on the fell that afternoon, but both brothers were summoned to appear before the County Petty Sessions for a breach of the Game Act.

At the trial, George, who had previously been up before the squire for poaching, agreed that he had been on Saddle Side as stated, but claimed he had gone there to check on the sheep which his father was licensed to put to graze on part of the fell. The bench found him guilty and fined him forty shillings, with costs. They dismissed the case against his brother, Charles.

LONGRIDGE

Longridge stands on the old road between Clitheroe and Preston. It derives its name (once spelt Longryche) from the three-mile long ridge leading to Jeffrey Hill and was previously just a local name for the joint townships of Alston and Dilsworth.

The Gunshot Mystery (1849)

When Isabella Taylor began an illicit relationship with Robert Walmsley, she had no idea of the trouble that she was creating for herself. Isabella was a live-in servant at the Longridge home of Revd William Charles Bache, where she met Walmsley, a married father of two children, when he came to work in the gardens. When she realised that she was probably pregnant with his child, Isabella broke the news and told her lover that she was going to a doctor in Preston to confirm her condition. When Walmsley told her that she had better not do this, as she would get them both in a 'hobble', Isabella replied that she would at least have to tell her employer, the Revd Bache.

At about 7 p.m. the following evening, as Isabella was clearing away the tea things, she lit a candle to take with her into the unlit pantry, which had only a small window. She had just put some plates on the shelf when something startled her, and as she turned around, she received a hail of gunshot in her face. The sheer force of the blast knocked her against the wall but she managed to stagger into the dining room to fall at the feet of the Revd's sister, Miss Bache. When Revd Bache arrived home about 9 p.m., he found the house in considerable commotion: although Isabella Taylor's wounds had been staunched, she was distraught and eventually confessed to her condition, naming Walmsley as the father of her unborn baby. Her employer sent for the police and when Constable William Durham arrived, he found a hole as large as an orange in the pantry window and about a hundred holes in the door opposite. After receiving information from the household members, PC Durham, accompanied by two men named Kenyon and Kay, went to Walmsley's home, which they found in darkness.

The constable stayed in the shadows whilst Kenyon knocked on the door and after about five minutes, Walmsley came to an upstairs window and asked, 'Who's there?' Kenyon told him to come out and heard him whispering to someone in the bedroom before he shouted down to ask if Kenyon had the police with him. Kenyon reiterated his request until Walmsley eventually came to the door. His wife was with him, and when she asked the constable why they had come for her husband, Walmsley shouted at her saying, 'What the hell is it to you; go to bed!' PC Durham arrested him, charging him with shooting and wounding his mistress, but he declared his innocence, willingly showing the officer his gun. He insisted that he had been at a sale at Hothersall at the time of the incident and had then called at the hall to collect tithe rates, not getting back home until almost 9 p.m.

When Walmsley stood trial for the shooting, no witnesses came forwards to corroborate his story but neither could anyone place him at the Bache house at the time of the shooting. The jury returned a verdict of not guilty, and he was immediately discharged.

Look, No hands! (1850)

When PC Denham received constant complaints about the conduct of carters on the Longridge Road, he decided to clean up his patch and brought several of them before the County Petty Sessions, charged with riding on their carts without reins. The bench was adamant that this risky behaviour should cease and fined one man ten shillings with costs, and ordered the rest to pay the costs incurred in bringing them to court.

LOWERHOUSE

'Big Bob' (1882)

In 1882, Lowerhouse was a district in its own right, not yet incorporated with the borough of Burnley. In May of the previous year, Robert Templeton arrived in the community to take up a job in the print works there. He was in his thirties, over 6ft tall, with a swarthy complexion. Despite his heavy drinking and offhand manner, the locals considered him a good worker. Templeton, or 'Big Bob' as he soon became known, found lodgings in Brook Row with Mrs Betty Scott, a thirty-three-year-old widowed mother of three children aged eleven, nine and five, who was expecting yet another child. She had two other lodgers at the time besides also looking after her twenty-three-year-old brother, who was crippled. Space in the house was at a premium so Big Bob at first shared a bedroom with the other lodgers, until his relationship with Betty developed into something more than that of landlady/lodger, when he moved into her bedroom, and her bed.

The couple's relationship quickly deteriorated, due in part to Templeton's excessive alcohol intake, and when his drinking cost him his job at the print works Betty, deciding she had had enough, moved into the back bedroom with her children. Her brother also had a single bed in the same room. By early 1882, Templeton's drinking had escalated to the point where he was making life at the house in Brook Row uncomfortable for the other residents, so Betty gave him notice to quit. Big Bob did not accept his former lover's decision, and after a full day of drinking in the local pubs with another lodger, he returned to the house in a foul temper, demanding his evening meal. Betty Scott was blazing at his behaviour and it showed in her attitude as she served his dinner. Templeton struck the table, accused her of treating him like a dog and then stomped upstairs to his bed.

An hour or so later, after everyone had retired for the night, Betty's brother saw Templeton enter the shared family bedroom and approach his sister. A short whispered argument followed, which ended with Betty ordering Big Bob back to his own room. At 3.30 a.m., the crippled man was still awake due to pain caused by his condition, and watched Templeton as he re-entered the room to lean briefly over the bed shared by mother and children before quietly retracing his steps. As the lodger left the bedroom, Betty made a strange guttural sound loud enough to wake the children. Her brother called her name, but receiving no reply he lowered himself off his bed and dragged his crippled body across the room, where he found a box of matches. The flame from a struck match was enough to show Betty lying on her side, blood oozing from a deep wound that crossed her throat. The children, by now sitting up in bed, were covered in their mother's blood, as were the bedclothes.

In the pandemonium that followed, Templeton paced nervously around the house, wearing only a vest and a pair of trousers. The police, who arrived swiftly at the scene, found a razor in his room and asked him to accompany them to Padiham police station. Big Bob went without protest.

The subsequent inquest, held at one of Templeton's regular haunts, the Bird in Hand, produced a coroner's verdict of wilful murder, as did a later magistrates hearing, and a trial at Manchester Assizes was set for 28 January.

Throughout his imprisonment and trial, Templeton did not deny the crime, but insisted that he could not remember it happening because of the large amount of alcohol he had consumed prior to the incident. The Assize jury took only forty-five minutes to reach a guilty verdict and the judge donned his black cap to deliver the death sentence. Several petitions for mercy were drawn up and presented on his behalf, but on 13 February 1882, Robert 'Big Bob' Templeton walked to his death on the scaffold at Strangeways Prison.

NELSON

Nelson grew up around the hamlets of Great Marsden and Little Marsden and was renamed in honour of Admiral Lord Nelson. Traces of the two Marsdens still linger in such legacies as Marsden Park and Marsden Hall, the sixteenth-century home of the Walton Family.

Bowling on the Highway (1877)
In March 1877, two unlucky fork makers, Alexander Faulkner and Joseph Heap, were the only culprits in a gathering of over 200 men to be arrested by plain-clothes policemen during an illegal session of bowling stones along the highway at Great Marsden. Nearby tenants had complained about the rowdy crowd gambling and carousing on a regular basis.

Alexander Faulkner denied the charge, saying that he could not have taken part in the game as he had a 'lame hand'. The officers testified that they had seen Faulkner bowling with his left hand, and he was found guilty and fined five shillings with costs. Joseph Heap admitted the offence and was fined one shilling.

Smash and Grab (1933)
When Albert Northcott, manager of Wraw's pawnbrokers, shut the lock-up shop at the close of business on Thursday 14 December 1933, he made sure that everything was secure before heading home for his evening meal. At 3.50 a.m. on Friday morning, the local 'bobby' checked the shop during his rounds and found nothing amiss. At 4.20 a.m. the same policeman saw a man he recognised as James Metcalfe driving his Overland Whippet saloon car, and noticed that he was carrying at least one passenger.

Marsden Hall.

As the car passed him, the officer saw that the rear number plate was not illuminated, so blew his whistle to indicate that Metcalfe should stop. Instead of complying, the car picked up speed and disappeared into the night. It was later found abandoned in the middle of Woodlands Road with the front and rear lights covered, and a poker, knife and joiner's tool on the floor.

The policeman, meanwhile, followed the car tracks back towards Leeds Road, where he found that a large stone had smashed the pawnbroker's plate glass window and the window display had been ransacked. When the manager, summarily roused from his bed, arrived at the scene, he reported that there were thirty-six gold and chromium wristwatches and fifty-one gold rings missing according to the stock book. These had a total value of £70 5s.

Following the bobby's nightly report, police arrested James Robert Metcalfe (twenty-eight) at his home on Leeds Road and two of his known associates – Frances Henry Mount (twenty-five), also of Nelson, and Robert Irving (forty) – a Bolton man. A few days later, two wedding rings and a gold wristwatch from the raid were recovered from a Manchester jeweller, who identified Irving as the person who had gone into his shop on 16 December and sold him the items for thirty-five shillings, using the name 'Kershaw'.

During the local hearing, and their subsequent trial at Salford Quarter Sessions on 22 and 23 January, the three men, who did not have legal representation, accused and counter-accused each other of the crime. Metcalfe described Irving's evidence as 'a concoction', whilst Mount declared that Irving 'ought to be an author' as he 'must have a marvellous memory, or else it is a false tale.' Irving, for his part, rounded on Metcalfe, saying, 'He is a monkey for giving me away.'

He then went on to suggest that the shop manager was trying to defraud the insurance company by claiming that the stolen goods were worth £70, when all that had been recovered was jewellery to the value of about £10.

The jury, however, seemed to accept that the three men had plotted the smash-and-grab raid together, purposely taking a large stone from Metcalfe's hen pen, which Mount threw through the pawnshop window before scooping whatever he could into his hat. Metcalfe kept his car engine running whilst Irving sat in the back seat with the door open ready for a quick getaway. They had abandoned the car and, whilst Metcalfe and Mount returned to their homes to establish alibis, Irving spent the night in Metcalfe's hen pen before catching a bus back to Bolton the next day taking the stolen jewellery with him.

The accused continued to protest their innocence and blame each other throughout the trial and summing up, but the jury found all three of them guilty as charged. After hearing that the men had previous criminal records, the judge sentenced Irving and Metcalfe to three years of penal servitude, and Mount to eighteen months of hard labour.

Pedalling Furiously (1933)

On a warm summer day in June 1933, twenty-two-year-old Maurice Simpson of Every Street was summoned before the police court and charged with 'furiously riding a pedal cycle' after Police Sergeant Rigg had witnessed him knocking down a Mrs Spiers in Hibson Road.

In his defence, Simpson countered that the sergeant had distracted him by waving his arms and shouting that he should slow down and it was because of this he had hit Mrs Spiers. The chairman of the bench, Mr W.E. Riley, told the court that 'the bench were of the opinion that the defendant rode the cycle recklessly and with disregard for the safety of the public'. He then fined Simpson twenty shillings.

A Callow Killing (1936)

On 22 June 1936, neighbours of Ruth Clarkson, a spinster in her seventies, were becoming concerned for her wellbeing as they had not seen her or heard her dog barking for several days. It was rumoured locally that although Miss Clarkson lived a squalid and apparently poverty-stricken existence, she was actually a wealthy property owner and had a horde of money and expensive jewellery hidden somewhere in her rubbish-strewn and rodent-infested terraced house.

On the same day, two detectives from Nelson police station – Detective Superintendent Linaker and Detective Chief Inspector Fenton – called at the spinster's house in Clayton Street after receiving information from a 'nark' that a dwarf had been selling quality pieces of jewellery to local pawnshops. The policemen knew of the rumours of Miss Clarkson's Victorian jewellery collection, and wanted to check that it was still in her possession.

Despite knocking loud and long at the door of No. 56, they failed to gain entry and one of the worried neighbours told the detectives that Miss Clarkson's niece, Edith Edmunson, had a key and lived nearby. They got the key and used it to go into the house via the back door, which appeared to have been forced open and then relocked from the outside with a key.

Even the two seasoned officers were shocked by what they found. Lying amongst a midden of old newspapers, discarded bottles and tins, and half-eaten food, was the spinster's raggedly dressed and blood-soaked body. Her head was split open in several places and her lower limbs were exposed, but she had obviously put up a fight, as there were also blood spatters on the walls and ceiling. Close to Ruth's lifeless form lay a heavy tyre lever, a section of iron railing, and a bloodstained plank, which the detectives presumed to be the murder weapons. Upstairs, they found Miss Clarkson's pet terrier hanging by its neck from a length of twine attached to a bedpost. The dog's body had already begun to putrefy, and was riddled with maggots.

Leaving the house guarded by several police constables, Linaker and Fenton went in search of their suspect. They knew of only one man in Nelson who was, in the terms of the time, classed as a dwarf – Max Mayer Haslam, a surly petty criminal who had only recently been released from Strangeways Prison, and frequented local pubs and lodging houses in company with a small group of Nelson's misfits and ne'er-do-wells. They came across him in Pendle Street where he was walking with unemployed labourer, Thomas Barlow, and when they later searched him at the police station found him to be carrying several items of jewellery and a key of the type missing from Miss Clarkson's house. Haslam insisted that he had owned the jewellery for a long time and the key was for the back door of his father's house in Heywood. The key proved not to fit any of the locks there, but when tried in the door of No. 56 Clayton Street, the lock opened without difficulty.

The police arrested Max Mayer Haslam for the murder of Miss Clarkson and he stood trial at Manchester Assizes on 8 December 1936. The trial, presided over by Mr Justice Lawrence, lasted for two days and a variety of witnesses gave evidence. Two of the most important prosecution witnesses were Thomas Barlow, who was with Haslam at the time of his arrest, and John William Davieson. Both these men stayed at the same Nelson boarding house as the accused, and were frequently in his company. They separately told the court that Haslam had admitted to killing Miss Clarkson and her dog and had shown them various items he had gained by his crime. Haslam also had a good deal of money, some of which he had used to buy drinks in the pub for his friends and later to pay for tickets for them to visit the picture house.

Barlow also testified that when the two detectives had stopped the pair on Pendle Street on 22 June 1936, Haslam had just offered him £200 to drive a body up to the swamp at Coldwell and throw it in.

Haslam's defence lawyers counter-claimed that Barlow and Davieson had gone to No. 56 Clayton Street a week before the murder to 'case the joint' and had returned themselves to rob and kill Miss Clarkson. Medical and forensic evidence, however, showed that Haslam had recent small fingernail scratches behind his ears and on his chest when his arrest took place, and a palm-print left on a bloodstained chair at the crime scene had matched a print taken from Haslam's right hand. He also had a possible dog-bite on his right index finger and traces of human blood were found on the toecap of his left boot. When faced with this evidence, Haslam replied, 'Not guilty. That's all I have to say.'

Having heard further evidence from a man claiming to have sold Haslam the tyre lever used in the killing, and having dismissed the accused man's alibi of being at a cricket match at the time of the offence, the jury took less than an hour to find him guilty of the murder of Ruth Clarkson.

Max Mayer Haslam was hanged at Strangeways Prison on 4 February 1937. An anti-hanging protest, led by Mrs van der Elst, took place outside the gaol whilst the execution took place, and at 9.15 in the morning, they played the hymn 'Nearer my God to Thee' as the officials posted the death notices for all to see.

NEWCHURCH-IN-PENDLE

Grave Robbing (1612)

The church of St Mary, Newchurch, built in 1544, has been altered and added to over the centuries. The only remaining original part is the tower, which bears a large blue/grey eye sculpted into its west face. This symbol represents the all-seeing eye of God and was meant to protect the villagers from evil. It was also there to deter local witches from stealing bones, teeth and other body parts from the graves to use in their remedies and potions. During the inquiries leading to the Pendle Witch trial of 1612, one of the accused, James Device – grandson of Old Demdike – showed some teeth to Yeoman Constable Henry Hargreaves that he claimed to have dug up from the graveyard at St Mary's to help in his witchcraft. He was later found guilty of witchcraft at Lancaster Castle and hanged.

At the same assizes, Jennet and Ellen Brierley were accused, but acquitted, of killing a baby by thrusting a nail into its navel in order to drink its blood. It was alleged that they later dug the child's body from its grave and rendered it into an ointment that helped them change form.

PADIHAM

Padiham lies on the river Calder, south of Pendle Hill, and was originally called Paddyngham. A settlement there dates back to before the Norman Conquest and Padiham was, for several centuries, a market town serving the whole of Pendleside. The town expanded rapidly during the Industrial Revolution, becoming a part of the borough of Burnley in the 1960s. Padiham Town Council was reinstated in 2002, but without much of the power formerly held by the Urban District Council of earlier years.

Salts of Lemon (1926)

At 4 a.m. on 6 July 1926, Richard Massey returned home to Hill Street Padiham, and told his mother, 'I have killed yon woman and I have taken poison.' Massey, who had lived with his mother since his wife's death a year before, had been away from home for three days, and his clothing was soaking wet.

The woman he referred to was Sarah Ellen Barker, a thirty-three-year-old married mother of three from Harle Syke. The two had been having an affair for quite some time and had recently found out that Sarah was pregnant. Her body was discovered in a Padiham beauty spot, Cockers wood. She was laying on her back, holding her gloves in one hand and a handkerchief in the other, her arms crossing her chest. The woman's hat lay on the trampled grass near to her body, as did a Guinness bottle, which contained traces of sediment.

Mr Barker had not seen his wife for three days, the last time being when he had left home for a day's haymaking at his brother's farm. He claimed he was not aware of his wife's affair, nor did he know that she was expecting another child. The fact that he had not reported his wife missing before the police took him news of the tragedy may suggest that their marriage was not a strong one and she was, perhaps, in the habit of staying away from home.

Massey, an ex-soldier, gave a rambling statement at Padiham police station during which he described a suicide pact he had agreed to at Sarah's insistence. During the three days they had spent living rough he claimed that she had talked constantly of committing suicide, refusing all his requests that she go home. She had finally driven him to agree to strangle her, before he was to drink the poison she had bought at a chemist's shop in Clayton-Le-Moors during their 'walkabout'. The poison was Salts of Lemon, used to remove mould and ink stains from clothing. It contained Oxalic acid, which can be fatal in large doses. Massey said that Sarah had told him she wanted to die, 'because I love you, Dick', describing how he had then strangled her and drunk the poison before going home.

He later amended his statement to tell how they had met in a local pub before going to Padiham Fair, where they stayed until it was time for Mrs Barker to take the last tram from Cheapside to Harle Syke. When the tram had pulled up Mrs Barker had refused to get on it, declaring that she was going to kill herself, so Massey had decided to stay with her to prevent this.

St Mary's church, Newchurch.

They walked for miles along the canal path and after buying the poison, they had returned to Padiham where they bought and drunk a bottle of Guinness. Sarah had then mixed the Salts of Lemon with a little water in the empty bottle. The couple then walked to the wood near Fennyfold Farm where they stopped to rest on the grass. Massey said he had told her there that he was not willing to go ahead with the suicide pact, whereupon Sarah had kissed him, picked up the bottle, and began drinking its contents. Massey's new story continued that he had accidentally killed his lover whilst trying to stop her taking the poison, and when he realised what he had done, he drank what was left in the bottle and fainted. He said he had 'never wanted her to die, and never intended to kill her.' He had come round some time later and crossed the woman's arms over her chest before leaving her lying on the grass.

It was this last statement that was used in Massey's defence during his trial at Lancaster Assizes on 23 October 1926, when medical evidence contradicted his version of events by indicating that the dead woman had not taken Salts of Lemon, or any other poison, before her death. Nevertheless, the jury retired for just eight minutes before reaching a unanimous verdict. They concluded that Massey was guilty of manslaughter rather than murder, because whilst he had caused her death, it was not a premeditated or deliberate act on his part. He was sentenced to three years of imprisonment.

PENDLE HILL

Pendle Hill is a common landmark of both the boroughs of Pendle and Ribble Valley. Standing 1,830ft at its highest point, the almost-mountain dominates the landscape for miles around. Its connections with the notorious Pendle Witches are well documented, and it was atop the hill's summit in 1652 that George Fox had a vision of God that led to his founding the Quaker movement. People who have long been proud to be 'Pendle folk', no matter on which borough, or side of the hill, they live, inhabit the many small villages nestled into the folds around its broad base.

Witchcraft (1612)

The word 'witch' comes from the Anglo-Saxon word '*Wicca*' (or '*wicce*'), which in turn is derived from an ancient Indo-European word meaning 'to bend, or to change'. Pendle Hill is famous as the home of the Pendle Witches, eleven poor uneducated men and women who stood trial at Lancaster Castle in 1612, charged with witchcraft.

The superstition surrounding witches in past centuries stemmed largely from ignorance, but some of these 'witches' used their reputations to their advantage. For instance, women with no real means of support would call at villages and isolated farmhouses begging for food or milk. Most people they asked would help if they could, because to refuse them would cause the women to curse and vilify them. It was inevitable that, due to the poor sanitation and living conditions of the time, occasionally someone who had been cursed would fall ill or die, or their children or cattle would suffer a similar fate. These misfortunes were then attributed to the work of the 'witch' who had issued the curse, causing them to be feared and, consequently, fed.

The arrest and subsequent trial of the Pendle Witches was instigated when a feud between two local families got out of hand. Ill feeling between the Southerns, headed by Elizabeth (Old Demdike), and Anne Whittle's (Chattox) brood had festered for years, so when Bessie Whittle wore clothing to church that she had stolen from the Demdike home at Malkin Tower, the Demdikes reported the theft to Roger Nowell of Read Hall. Nowell was a local justice of the peace and saw the opportunity of ridding himself of the troublesome families by encouraging them in their claims and counter-claims against each other. The accusations escalated to claims of murder by witchcraft, and eventually eleven Pendle people found themselves imprisoned in Lancaster Castle.

Old Demdike died in the gaol before the assizes began and so escaped the harrowing ordeal that the other wretches suffered. The fates of these were as follows:

Found Guilty and Hung – Anne Whittle, Anne Redfearn, Elizabeth Device, James Device, Alison Device, Alice Nutter, Katherine Hewitt (Mouldheels).

Found NOT Guilty and Hung – John Bulcock and his wife, Jane Bulcock.

Acquitted – Alice Gray.

At the same assizes, Isobel Roby of Windle was found guilty of a separate charge of witchcraft and sentenced to death by hanging, whilst Margaret Pearson of Padiham was found guilty of witchcraft and sentenced to a term of imprisonment and time in the pillory. Six further individuals, who came to be known as the 'Salmesbury Witches', also faced the court, but were acquitted. These were – Elizabeth Astley, Jennet Brierley, Ellen Brierley, Laurence Haye, Isabel Sidegreaves and Jane Southworth. For more about witches see *Witches and Ghosts Of Pendle and the Ribble Valley,* also written by Jacqueline Davitt and published by Tempus Publishing.

Pendle Hill – a Ribble Valley view.

Opposite above: Pendle Hill from above Roughlee.

Opposite below: Pendle Hill from the borough of Pendle.

THE PILLORY

The pillory was a popular form of punishment from the sixteenth to the early nineteenth centuries, as it was a stipulation that all towns with a market licence must have one. They were used to hold petty criminals such as vagabonds, beggars, adulterers and drunks, whose limbs (usually the arms) would be inserted through holes in two wooden boards which were then locked together to hold them fast. Although the miscreant would only be held this way for a few hours, it was a harsh punishment as during this time they would be the subject of derision and abuse from the townspeople. Depending on the prisoner's crime, sometimes displayed on a board, the crowd would hurl anything from mouldy turnips and rotten eggs to dead cats and large stones at their target and, because of the way in which the pillory held them fast, the offenders could not protect their exposed bodies from this onslaught. Sometimes a further punishment, such as branding, would be meted out during a criminal's time in the pillory.

QUAKERS

As mentioned earlier, it was whilst on the summit of Pendle Hill in 1652 that George Fox had the vision which inspired him to form the Quaker movement. It followed that the Quakers built up a strong and loyal membership in the area and in 1600, when King Charles II returned to claim his throne his government feared that many hostile and disillusioned soldiers would join them, as the sect was strictly anti-monarchical.

The Clarendon code sought to re-impose loyalty to Church and State and provided for the prosecution of Quakers and members of other revolutionary sects. Almost 300 Lancashire men, women and children were incarcerated in stinking prisons for their beliefs and the ensuing 'crimes' of refusing the oath, disrupting church services, and attending secret meetings. One such man, James Whipp of Twiston near Downham, faced proceedings at least seven times in eleven years. These are his 'crimes':

1660 – Committed to prison for refusing the oath
1665 – For having private Quaker meetings at his house
1665 – For not attending Divine Service on Sundays and holidays
1668 – Arrested for attending a secret meeting at a house in Padiham - sent to prison and fined thirty-six shillings
1668 – Excommunicated and sent to gaol
1670 – For not bringing his wife and child to be buried at the chapel, but burying them in the field
1671 – For keeping monthly conventicles in his house

REEDLEY HALLOWS

Martyrs (1600)
Following Henry VIII's marriage to Anne Boleyn, he passed various acts of parliament which did away with Papal Authority and which made it a treasonable offence to deny the validity of his union with Anne, or to deny his position as supreme head of the Church. Queen Elizabeth I, a staunch Protestant, passed laws during her reign prohibiting the Roman Catholic mass, making attendance at Protestant Church services mandatory and proscribing the death sentence for

anyone breaking these laws. Execution was also the punishment for anyone found to be a priest or any persons caught helping or hiding a priest.

During this period of Catholic persecution, Pendle and the Ribble Valley had a strong alliance of Roman Catholic families who refused to give up their faith, and were forced to practise in secret. Travelling priests would visit their houses and communities to administer the Mass and other rites, and the grander houses often had hidden priest holes used to conceal the men of the Church when Protestant officials came looking for them.

One such priest, Robert Nutter, lived for a time at Laund House, Reedley Hallows, with his brother John. According to local legend, Anne Whittle, known as Chattox and executed with her fellow Pendle Witches in 1612, was a frequent visitor to the brothers' home and to nearby Greenhead Farm.

John, also a priest, was hung at Tyburn in 1584, whilst Robert was severely tortured in the dungeons there before being put aboard the ship *Mary Martin* and banished to Europe with several other priests. He returned to England using the name Robert Rowley but was arrested in London and imprisoned once more. Robert eventually managed to escape, making his way back north to continue his work in the priesthood. He was arrested again, this time facing trial at Lancaster Castle, where he was found guilty before being hung, drawn and quartered on 26 July 1600.

RIBCHESTER

Although Ribchester is most famous for its Roman remains, Bronze Age artefacts have also been found at the site. In the eighteenth century, the village housed many handlooms and some of the weavers' three-storey cottages still remain in the centre of the village.

Murder at the Setters Arms (1862)

The Setters Arms, an alehouse in Fleet Lane, Ribchester, was actually the living room of Annie Walne's cottage. The elderly widow, who had been born in 1783, had no other income apart from the few shillings she managed to raise by selling the dairy produce that she made from milk produced by her small herd of cows. Her customers were mainly locals who would gather there from the remote valley farms, supplemented by staff from the Ribchester workhouse and occasional travellers on the road between Preston and Blackburn.

Joseph Ward was the labour master at the workhouse in 1862 and had known Anne Walne for many years, often calling at her cottage for a pint of beer in the evenings. The two had become firm friends over time and as Annie's health began to fade with her advancing years, Ward had taken over the chore of feeding and milking the widow's cows most mornings.

On the morning of 11 September 1862, he called at the cottage as usual and found the place in darkness. Although this was unusual, Annie being an early riser, Ward was not unduly worried as she had been well and in good spirits when she had served him his ale on the previous evening. He went about his tasks and when he had finished, he approached the cottage to check that all was okay. On reaching the front door, he saw that the key was on the outside of the lock and, unable to raise a reply from Annie, he turned it and pushed the door. The door would not budge more than an inch or two because something heavy had been wedged up against it, so Joseph raced around to the back of the cottage. There he found that the entire window and its frame had been wrenched from the wall and was now lying in the garden. Shouting again to Annie, and still receiving no reply, he decided there had been a robbery and went to get help.

Ward soon returned with local farmer William Pye, and the two men entered the cottage through the hole where the window had been. Once inside they saw that drawers had been

Almshouses, Ribchester.

emptied and their contents had been scattered willy-nilly about the room, so fearing for Annie's safety they climbed the stairs to her bedroom. The old woman lay spread-eagled on her bed, her hands tied to the bedposts with handkerchiefs and naked from the waist down. Her shawl tightly covered her face and the bed was covered in blood. The men fetched Sergeant Whiteside from the village, who discovered two more handkerchiefs tied tightly around the victim's neck.

The sergeant returned to his office and telegraphed for senior officers to attend the scene. These duly arrived on horseback, in the persons of Superintendent McNab from Blackburn and Superintendent Green from Preston. Whiteside suggested that a local man named Thomas Davis was a likely suspect and the senior officers arrested him; after interrogations, they were unable to find any evidence to implicate him in the killing, and they had to free him after the coroner's inquest declared that Annie Walne 'had been murdered by some person or persons unknown.'

At this point, the case seemed to have grown cold until £100 was offered as a reward for evidence or information leading to the arrest and conviction of the killer. This large sum quickly drew the attention of a gamekeeper at Salmesbury named Thomas Bowling, who himself had convictions for poaching and burglary. Known as 'Chorley Tom', the gamekeeper named five men: Duncan McPhail, Benjamin Hartley, Daniel Carr and brothers George and William Woods. The police arrested these men on Monday 1 December. They also arrested Bowling, but soon let him go.

One of the five, Benjamin Hartley, was more than ready to confess to his part in the crime. He described how, a few days before the robbery, Duncan McPhail had told him that he knew of an old woman who ran a beerhouse in Ribchester and had recently sold one of her cows, so must have money. Together with Carr and George Woods, they had made their way from

Blackburn to Ribchester with the intention of robbing the woman. He told how George Woods was carrying a crowbar and a stick, Carr a cane with a piece of lead attached to it by copper wire, and McPhail a crowbar and a loaded pistol. Hartley claimed that he was the only one of the motley crew not to be armed. It had been a rough, arduous journey, and the night stormy with showers of heavy hailstones. They had stopped in a barn to rest and drink rum, and when they had finally reached the Setters Arms, they had waited in an outbuilding until they were sure that all was quiet at the cottage.

Hartley said that McPhail had been the ringleader and had ordered him to keep watch whilst the others removed the kitchen window and entered the cottage. He had then joined them and gone upstairs, where they found Annie Walne in her bed. They asked her where she kept her money but she started screaming so he had held her down to silence her. It had been Dan Carr who had struck the old woman on the head with his weighted cane and George Woods who had tied her to the bed with handkerchiefs whilst Carr and McPhail continued rummaging around the bedroom. Annie was still alive and moaning at this point. Hartley confessed that each got £4 10s 6d from the money they eventually discovered and whilst McPhail and George Woods had caught a train to Bamber Bridge after fleeing the scene, he and Dan Carr had gone for a drink in a Preston pub before catching an early morning train to Cherry Tree station, near Blackburn.

Following his confession, Superintendents Green and McNab took Hartley to Ribchester where he showed them the barn in which they had rested on the night of the crime. There were many footprints in the earth floor, which the police officers took pains to preserve for evidence. Hartley then took them on the route he had described, pointing out the spot where McPhail had thrown away his crowbar. It was still there and, when it was measured against marks made on the removed window frame at the Setters Arms, it was clearly the tool used to remove it. Several witnesses substantiated Hartley's version of events, and Carr's cane was found and identified as being consistent with the weapon that had been used to strike Annie Walne.

Carr, McPhail and George Woods were brought before the magistrates and committed for trial at the next Assizes, but, in view of his cooperation, Hartley was not to be tried with them. Nothing whatsoever was found to implicate George Woods' brother, William, who Chorley Tom had also named, and he walked free. On the morning of the Assize trial, Daniel Carr died in his cell; so of the five originally accused of the widow's murder, just two of them stood trial.

Duncan McPhail had previously been transported for seven years for perjury and had returned to Blackburn on a ticket of leave. George Woods was a joiner. Both men had visited Annie Walne's beerhouse and had boots that were of the type that had left footprints in the Ribchester barn. Chorley Tom (Bowling) gave evidence that McPhail had admitted to him that he had organised the robbery. Elements of Hartley's statement held water, although the police surgeon (Dr William Hartland) gave evidence that that even though Mrs Walne's head wounds had been serious, the cause of her death was suffocation due to the handkerchiefs stuffed in her mouth and held firmly by the tight shawl around her body.

The rest of the evidence against the two remaining men was either very flimsy or at best circumstantial, but the statements given by Hartley and Bowling were given unusual credit by the judge, Mr Baron Martin. After lengthy consideration the jury pronounced a verdict of guilty against both McPhail and Woods, with a recommendation for mercy. The judge declared that he found it difficult to imagine why such 'ruffians' be spared and donned the black cap to pronounce sentence of death on the pair.

Benjamin Hartley, who was formally acquitted, fled in fear of his life when large crowds beset his house, baying for his blood. On Sunday 26 April 1863, McPhail and Woods were hanged at Kirkside Gaol. Neither man confessed to the attending chaplain, with a large crowd witnessing their last moments.

THE SCOLD'S BRIDLE

A scold in Middle English was the term used for a shrewish, ribald or abusive woman who annoyed others by constantly finding fault, or being a nuisance to her family or neighbours. A punishment used for such troublesome women, thought to originate in Europe and brought to Britain during the seventeenth century, was the scold's bridle, or 'brank'.

This device was a type of iron cage for the head that had a sharpened or spiky plate attached to the inside. This protuberance fitted into the scold's mouth so that if she tried to talk or move her tongue she risked serious injury. Town officials would then parade the encumbered woman through the streets, sometimes leading her by a rope or chain, where the gathered crowds would ridicule the scold, sometimes even pelting her with rotten food – or worse!

SLAIDBURN

The village of Slaidburn sits on the banks of the river Hodder amidst the moorland of the Forest of Bowland. Its 'Hark to Bounty' inn dates back to the thirteenth century and Oliver Cromwell reputedly used the inn's Moot Courtroom during the Civil War. The village also boasts a fifteenth-century church, whose history is traceable to even earlier times.

The Child in the Stream (1855)

At about 7 p.m. on Sunday 17 May 1885, Farmer Bargh and his wife discovered the body of a young child in a stream a little way on the road from Slaidburn to Bolton-by-Bowland. The following day two sisters, Grace Isherwood and Isabella Gardener, were taken into custody on suspicion of being involved in the child's death. Following an inquest at the Black Bull Inn, Slaidburn, which reached a verdict of wilful murder, the women appeared before the Magistrate's Court at Bolton-by-Bowland and from there went to trial at Leeds Assizes to face a charge of murdering a little boy, Thomas Gardener.

The sisters hailed originally from Dalton-in-Furness, but Grace had secured the post of housekeeper to a widowed farmer named Isherwood at Meanley farm, Newton, near Slaidburn and after a few months in his employ, she became his wife. Prior to her marriage, Grace had borne two illegitimate children, the younger living with her at the farm and another, a boy of about two and a half years old, who she had left with a minder in her hometown. A disagreement about payment for the child's care arose and this resulted in Grace's sister, Isabella Gardener, bringing her nephew to the farm at Slaidburn.

Mrs Isherwood was afraid that the revelation of another illegitimate child might cause her husband to throw her out, so she told him that the child's name was Thomas Dockray and that Isabella was nursing him for his mother Elizabeth Dockray. The farmer, although somewhat suspicious, allowed them to stay, but his attitude began to change towards his wife until she began to fear for her position. After about a week or so, the sisters borrowed a neighbour's pony and cart and took Thomas to Clitheroe Union workhouse. The matron refused to take the child as they had no admittance order from the local relieving officer and turned them away. The women drove back to the farm where Grace went inside to tell her husband that they were going to take Thomas to his mother and then she followed Isabella along the road towards Langcliffe Cross Bridge. A neighbour, Mrs Tomlinson, who had witnessed this, asked Isabella about Thomas the following day and Isabella confirmed that they had returned him to his mother.

When Mr and Mrs Bargh found the child's body, he was lying face down in about 18in of water near to Langcliffe Cross Bridge. He was wearing two petticoats and a shirt, but no hat or

Right: A scold bridled.

Below: Scold's bridle.

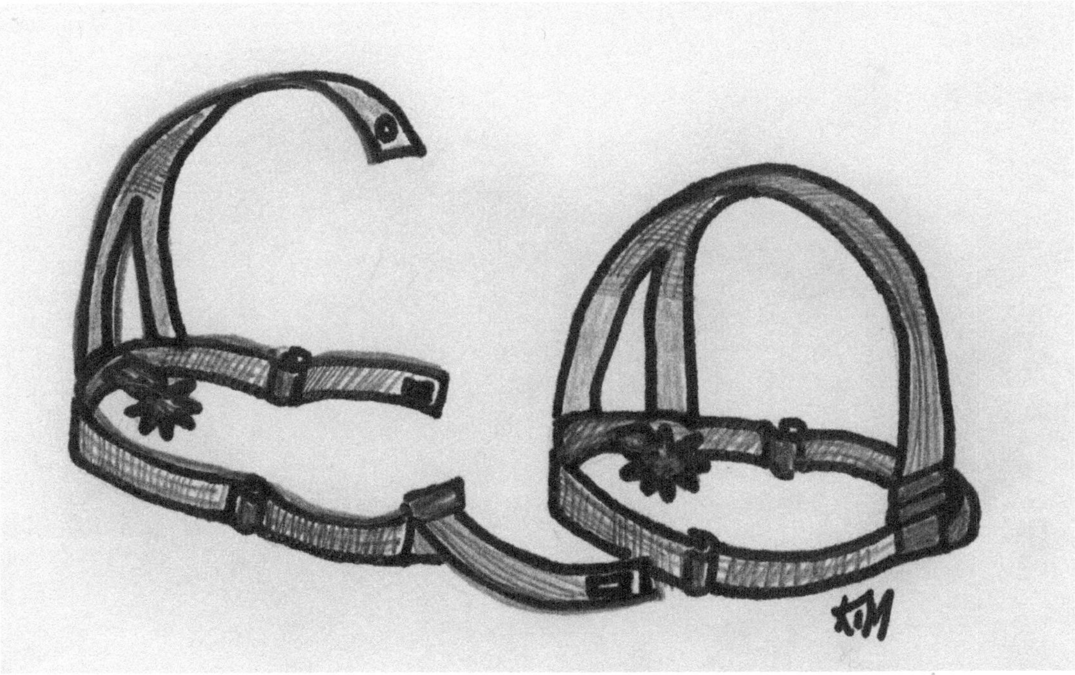

Hark to Bounty.

Rough moorland on the road between Slaidburn and Clitheroe.

The old court room at the Hark to Bounty.

coat. These garments were later found at Meanly Farm and identified as those worn by the child known as Thomas Dockray. Investigations then ensued that proved that the child in the stream was in fact Grace's son, Thomas Gardener. The surgeon who made the post-mortem report attributed the death to asphyxia by drowning, a verdict that both women hotly disputed.

Isabella read a written statement to the jury in which she admitted that the child was her sister's, but claimed that his death was accidental. According to her testimony, the sisters had decided to tell Grace's husband the truth after they had been sent away from the workhouse door. They had wrapped the child in rugs to keep him warm on the journey home, but when they arrived back at the farm, and lifted him out of the cart, he fell to the ground 'as though it were dead.' They did not dare to take the child into the house in case the farmer thought they had harmed it, so they decided to cover their tracks with a 'cock and bull' story. The sisters then went along the road towards the bridge, where they put the body into the water, after first removing his coat and hat.

The prosecution argued that it was unlikely that rugs on such a journey would suffocate a healthy child of Thomas' age without the women noticing something amiss. The defence lawyer countered this by pointing out that Grace and Isabella would have had plenty of opportunity to kill and hide the boy somewhere less obvious if they had planned and carried out the deed. He also claimed that undigested food in Thomas' stomach was conclusive evidence that death had taken place before his body went into the stream.

The Assize judge took an hour to sum up, and the jury just forty-five minutes to reach a 'not guilty' verdict. The crowded courtroom erupted with applause as the women walked free, but the throng waiting outside were of a different mind and hooted in derision as the sisters left the building.

'Big Jack' (1883)

In 1883, the quiet village of Slaidburn was, as a newspaper of the time described it, 'the scene of a tragic occurrence'. Mary Simpson, a respectable widow, was found lying dead behind the door of her bedroom at Town End. From her appearance, foul play was immediately suspected and police soon arrested an Irishman living in Clitheroe in connection with her death. The man, John Purcell, was known to have lodged with Mrs Simpson and had been seen visiting her house on the afternoon of her death. He was a master drainer who, being over 6ft tall with curly brown hair and a handsome face, was known locally as 'Big Jack'. Forty-year-old Purcell was a quiet, well thought of figure in the area, but he could become extremely belligerent when under the influence of alcohol.

At the inquest into Mary Simpson's death, held at the Hark to Bounty Inn, several witnesses gave testimony to having seen Big Jack in Slaidburn on the day of the incident. John Thomas Parker, the village postman, told how he had seen the Irishman drinking in the Hark to Bounty just after 1 p.m. Purcell was wearing a red checked jacket and a brown cap 'with neb and ears', and was drinking hard. When he left the inn about 2.40 p.m., he asked Parker to give him a lift into Clitheroe and the postman agreed to pick him up at Mary Simpson's house when he was ready to leave. Parker told the inquest that he had arrived at the house at about 3.10, and leaving his horse and cart by the gate, he had gone up the path to shout, 'are you coming?' to Purcell through the open front door. When Purcell joined him two or three minutes later, he noticed that his passenger was wearing a different cap to that which he had worn in the pub. He also noticed that his face was bleeding: Purcell told him that he had made his nose bleed by 'tumbling', after which comment he remained silent and sullen for the rest of the journey.

PC Nolan, the constable stationed at Town End, then recounted how he had visited Mrs Simpson's house around 5.25 p.m. the same day, at the request of Phoebe Carr, a neighbour who suspected all was not well. They found the door still open and went into the house together, where they found Mary's still-warm body in a bedroom. She was dressed, but her clothing was in disarray and bloodstained. The constable sent for Dr Seabrook, and when the body was lifted onto the bed they found Big Jack's cap with its 'neb and ears' on the floor where she had lain. The widow's hands were covered in blood and there was blood on the bedroom door. Dr Seabrook judged that she had been dead for between two and three hours, and he had been unable to find any cuts or bruises on her body. The doctor also confirmed in his evidence that the bloody marks that the postman had seen on Purcell's face were most probably fingernail scratches.

The coroner summed up before instructing the jury that they must decide whether any violence had been involved in the woman's death and, if they felt that to be the case, it was their duty to send anyone they thought to be involved to answer for Mary Simpson's death. After twenty minutes of deliberation, the jury returned a verdict of manslaughter against John 'Big Jack' Purcell.

STOCKS

The use of stocks as a punishment can be traced back to medieval times, when they were popular as a restraining device for minor criminals. The punishment was meant to humiliate the offender, whose ankles would be locked through two holes in the middle of a wooden plank, often barefoot, whilst being subject to a barrage of verbal abuse by the mocking crowd. The felon had to endure his term of punishment however bad the weather and would receive only bread and water for sustenance. Sometimes friends or family would bring food to them, but other less friendly visitors would throw rubbish at the prisoner, or torture and tease them by tickling

Sent to the stocks. (courtesy of Lancashire Library and Information Services)

their feet. Being unable to retaliate, the prisoner would have to endure whatever humiliation his neighbours dished out, although I'm sure they must have spent some of their time in the stocks remembering the names and faces of their worst tormentors for future reference.

In his 1929 publication *Annals and Stories of Barrowford*, Jessie Blakey tells how, many years before, one villager, Joseph Starkie (then aged sixteen), spent three hours on a Saturday morning locked in the stocks in front of Colne church, guarded by a policeman. One of eleven children, Starkie had been playing marbles near some boys who had been playing a game with coins. A policeman had come upon the scene and had arrested him for gambling. He was fined a few shillings but his father, convinced of his son's innocence, refused to pay – so the lad ended up in the stocks.

Blakey reports that 'he seems to have rather enjoyed the experience, whilst his mother treated it as a good joke.' The passing crowds must have been in good humour that day!

TRANSPORTATION

The transportation of felons across the sea took place as early as the seventeenth century when James I ordered such criminals to be sent to a life of almost-slavery in the plantations of the East Indies and other British colonies. In 1679, an act of parliament was passed which set out the various crimes, once punishable by death, which could be commuted to transportation. These ranged from treason, rape and murder, to sheep stealing and the sending of threatening letters.

Most of those transported were men, with only about one in six being female, and this discrepancy added to unrest and dissatisfaction of many of the prisoners, both on board ship and in the new colonies.

The first batch of prisoners transported to the new colony of Australia in 1788 comprised almost 600 criminals. Amongst them were thirteen-year-old Elizabeth Youngson and her twelve-year-old brother George, the youngest felons ever to be transported from Lancaster Castle. The siblings had received death sentences for breaking into a silk warehouse and stealing a jar of money, which held less than £2.50 in today's money. In 1831, over 3,000 felons made the journey from Great Britain to the Antipodes, but by the mid-nineteenth century, the colonies were assuming a mantle of respectability and were becoming increasingly reluctant to admit transportees. At the same time, the authorities at home were beginning to realise that transportation was no longer acting as a deterrent as many of the poor saw it as a way to a better life.

At the height of the transportation system prisoners were divided into classes according to their behaviour. If they acted in an exemplary manner, they could be granted a Ticket of Leave after eighteen months, which would give them the right to work in 'Van Dieman's Land' and follow whatever trade they had learned during their imprisonment. Prisoners who behaved badly were sent to Tasmania following their prison term, where they had to work in building gangs without payment, and without the company of their families.

The voyage to Australia from Great Britain took eight or nine months with only two ports of call on route to collect provisions and make repairs. Life was arduous on board and many convicts died during the voyage.

TRAWDEN

In the fourteenth century, the land around Trawden consisted of a few vaccaries, the forerunners of cattle farms, owned by the lord of the manor and worked by tenants. It was not until the sixteenth century that the tenants became owners of the copyhold and began to drain and cultivate the land for arable use, building farmsteads and cottages for themselves.

Coalmines existed around Trawden until the late nineteenth/early twentieth century and the cotton industry had a firm foothold in the village during 'King Cotton's' hey-day.

A Curious Incident at Hollin Hall (circa 1840)
In his book *The Annals of Trawden Forest* (1922), Fred Bannister recounts a tale of a shooting that took place at Hollin Hall some seventy or eighty years earlier. It concerns a man who hated his nickname

Having nothing better to do with their time and enjoying the effect it had on their victim, a group of boys would stand outside this man's house and shout out his hated nickname (which Bannister does not mention). The man would dash out of the house on hearing their taunts and chase the ne'er-do-wells hoping to catch and punish them. Being younger and quicker on their feet the boys always managed to escape, sometimes further taunting him by stopping to wait until he almost had them in his grasp before running away again.

One evening when the boys began their cruel game, the man shouted to them that he had a loaded gun and would shoot them if they carried on with their name-calling. The boys swiftly disappeared into the night, but were back to their old tricks after dark on the next day. Seizing his gun, the man chased them along Hollin hall and over the slope of Cock Hill, where one of the boys stood egging him on. The man shouted a warning, and then fired a shot. The boy fell to the ground, apparently dead.

Hollin Hall. (courtesy of Lancashire Library and Information Services)

Bannister goes on to describe how the man went home to his wife, who suggested that they bury the lad's body to escape punishment. He agreed, so they lit a lantern and set out to retrieve the corpse. When they reached the spot where the boy had fallen, they found to their amazement that the 'body' was made of straw!

A Fleeting figure (1941)
When the dressmaking class at Colne Technical School finished on the evening of 25 March 1941, Eileen Barrett headed to the bus stop at the junction of Albert Road and Linden Road, leaving her friend, Elizabeth Kelsall, chatting to classmates.

Eileen, an innocent nineteen year old from Trawden, had been working as a cashier and secretary at the Royal Assurance offices in Burnley for the past two years and was used to catching the bus home alone from there and from her evening class. The night of the 25th was particularly dark due to the heavy rain that was falling and to the blackout regulations that were in force during the war years.

When Eileen reached the bus stop, she got into a conversation with a man who told her that he too was waiting for a bus. The man then grabbed her by the throat. As she felt him hit her hard in her back, she screamed for help. Robert Duerden, a local fitter and turner, heard her scream as he walked up Albert Road. At first, he could not tell from which direction the cry had come and shouted, 'Are you all right?' He then turned back and saw Miss Barrett standing under a lamppost. He did not see anyone else in the immediate area, nor did he hear the footsteps of anyone running away. He rushed towards the girl and repeated his question, whereupon she told him what had happened. The postmaster, George Keith, arrived at the scene at this point and the two men helped the frightened girl onto a bus. Mr Keith said later that he had seen a 'fleeting figure' going down Linden Road.

Rear view of the technical school.

During the short journey to the bus station, where she was due to change buses, Eileen became quite ill. Mr Keith described how she had kept 'putting back her head and moaning' and when he went to her assistance he put his hand on her back to steady her and discovered that she was bleeding badly.

Miss Barrett was rushed to Hartley Hospital, where she was found to have a 5in-deep stab wound between her spine and shoulder blade, which had pierced her lung and severed a large blood vessel leading to the heart. Because of this injury, she haemorrhaged and died the same evening.

An inquest reached a verdict of 'murder by some person or persons unknown', and an extensive police enquiry was initiated, led by Detective Chief Superintendents Kenton and Gregson, ably assisted by a team of at least twenty other detectives. Between them, they interviewed all students and staff who had been at the Technical School on the night of the murder, traced, and interviewed a further 200 people who were at a Co-operative whist drive and dance being held at the Municipal Hall on the same evening. The team also visited all the cotton mills in Colne, Nelson, and outlying villages, conducted house-to-house inquiries throughout the area, and checked all local mental institutions in their quest for a suspect.

The only lead to emerge was that a fifteen-year-old girl came forward to say that on the night before Miss Barrett's murder, a man who had asked if her name was Gladys had attacked her at Reedley. The police team interviewed all local women and girls with that name to see if a connection could be established, but as with their other lines of inquiry nothing emerged to help solve the mystery.

TURF MOOR

Football Hooliganism (1897)

It seems that football hooliganism is not a new phenomenon, although the missiles thrown onto the pitch or aimed at players may have changed over the years and are more likely to be coins or mobile phones than stones. This report copied from *The Nelson Times* of 12 April 1897 describes just such an incident and the punishment doled out to the culprit may explain why football hooliganism was far less prominent in days gone by.

THE ASSAULT ON A FOOTBALLER AT BURNLEY – Throwing a clinker at a player.

At the Burnley Borough Police Court, Hillary Griffiths, one of the Wolverhampton Wanderers half-backs, summoned Richard Smout, who did not appear, for assault. Mr C.E. Sutcliffe, who appeared for the complainant, said that it was a case which was fortunately of a very rare occurrence. It arose at Turf Moor on the 20th inst, when Burnley were playing Wolverhampton Wanderers, and during the course of the match the complainant was struck on the head with a clinker, which was thrown by the defendant. That sort of thing was a very serious matter, and as far as the club were concerned, they had been most anxious to ascertain who threw the stone. He would be able to satisfy the bench, beyond the slightest shadow of doubt, that the defendant threw it.

Hillary Griffiths said he followed the occupation of a brass-caster as well as playing football. He took part in the match against Burnley on the 20th inst, and was struck on the back of the head by a stone, but he did not know who threw it. He had not been able to follow his employment since.

Joseph Whittaker, hotel proprietor, said he was on the stand right opposite to where the stone was thrown. The defendant threw the stone, and he asked him what he had done it for. The man looked at him and ran away. Witness saw the stone strike Griffiths.

George Thornton also spoke to seeing the stone thrown. He ran after the man. His name was Richard Smout, and he was known by some people as 'Shropshire Dick.'

After a brief consultation, the Bench said the defendant would be committed to prison for a month with hard labour.

WEST BRADFORD

The village of West Bradford, about two miles from Clitheroe, existed before the writing of the Domesday Book. In the fourteenth century, it had thirty-two inhabitants, who were mostly labourers.

Found Drowned (1871)

A headline in the *Preston Guardian* of 11 February 1871 read, 'Supposed Wife Murder near Clitheroe'. It went on to tell how husband and wife, John and Alice Morley, were heard arguing as they passed through Clitheroe on their way from Blackpool to their home at West Bradford. Witnesses heard Alice exclaim, 'Do you want to murder me and the children too?', but dismissed it at the time as being a matter of domestic bickering. Later that afternoon, a thirteen-year-old girl, Mary Elizabeth Titterington, found a woman's bonnet, umbrella and shawl near to the long bridge across the river Ribble over which the Morleys would have had to pass to reach home. These effects were identified as belonging to Alice Morley, and a search along the river

The bridge at West Bradford.

for signs of the woman began. After two hours, searchers found Alice's body. The rain-swollen waters had swept it down river until it had reached Waddington Brook foot where it washed up. The woman who came to lay out the corpse at the Morley home reported it to be neither bruised nor battered, nor were Alice's clothes torn or displaced. Some black markings, however, did appear on the dead woman's right arm before her burial.

A further search of the river and its banks did not reveal any sighting of John Morley and rumour concerning the drowning ran rife amongst the locals. Some were of the opinion that John Morley had murdered his wife before fleeing to escape punishment, whilst others thought that some mishap had occurred to them both and John's body would also come out of the river at some time. The coroner at Alice's inquest returned a verdict of 'Found Drowned' and issued a warrant for the arrest of John Morley on a charge of murder.

By mid-March, the water level in the Ribble had fallen dramatically and the police decided to carry out a further search. They dragged the riverbed until they found what they were looking for 150 yards upstream from the weir at Waddow: John Morley's body was badly decomposed after six weeks in the water and it was not clear whether an abrasion on his nose had been caused before or after his death. His clothes, like those of his wife, were untorn and his pockets contained a knife, a tobacco box, a three-penny piece, a halfpenny, a woman's hairnet and a two-foot rule. Again, the coroner's verdict was one of 'Found Drowned', but the exact circumstances surrounding the two deaths have never emerged.

WHALLEY

Whalley's famous abbey is said to be haunted by the ghost of Abbot Paslew. Cistercian monks, led by Abbot Gregory of Norbury, erected the edifice in the thirteenth century.

A Whalley Martyr (1676)

John Thules, the son of a schoolmaster, grew up in the Ribble Valley before becoming ordained into the priesthood in 1592. He conducted secret masses and administered holy offices in the area and throughout England, hidden and protected by his devout followers for many years before his arrest at the home of a Chorley weaver, Roger Wrenno. Thules and his host were imprisoned in Lancaster Castle and, after a futile escape attempt, were sent to the gallows there.

At their joint execution, both men were offered an immediate pardon if they would recant, with the priest receiving the added incentive of £20 per year for life. They refused to disown Papal authority and recognise the king as supreme head of the Church so were hung, drawn and quartered on 18 March 1616.

His executioners mounted John Thule's head on a spike above the gate of Lancaster Castle, whilst other parts of his body were on display at strategic points of the county as a warning to other practising Roman Catholics.

Another, earlier, Whalley martyr was Abbot John Paslew, the last abbot of Whalley Abbey, who refused to give up the abbey to Henry VIII or to swear allegiance to the king as supreme head of the Church. He was executed for high treason in 1537, and his ghost is said to haunt his beloved abbey to this day.

Police Brutality (1844)

When Thomas Burns, a hawker of brushes from Blackburn, went into The Shoulder of Mutton public house, Whalley, at about 9 p.m. and was unable to book a bed for the night, he asked the landlord where he could find a policeman. He thought he was in luck when the landlord told him that Constable Malcolm Graham was drinking in the pub, and pointed him out. The policeman suggested that Burns try The Swan Inn, which was just across the street, and agreed to meet him there in a few minutes to see if he had been successful.

The Swan was also full, so Constable Graham took Burns to a nearby lodging house where they were met with a similar story. This appeared to agitate the constable, who pushed Burns through the door, the salesman's brushes rattling with the force of the shove. He then swore at the hawker, telling him, 'I'll find you lodgings, and make you pay dear for them!' The policeman then knocked the man down, striking him several times and causing his eye to swell up. Burns called out, 'Murder, murder!', and bystanders later confirmed that Graham had continued to abuse the injured man, before dragging him by the collar across the street to the house where he had his own lodgings. After handcuffing his hapless prisoner, he bundled him into a gig, taking him to the Clitheroe lock-up, where he kept him all night.

The next day, Constable Graham took his prisoner before Revd P. Abbott, when he laid charges against Burns of assault on a policeman and being drunk and disorderly. No one would corroborate the policeman's story and several reliable witnesses gave evidence that Burns had been sober, orderly and unresisting at the time of his arrest. The magistrates believed the hawker's version of events and severely censured Graham for his 'gross conduct and cruelty', ordering him to pay the costs of the case. They then, however, took the highly unusual step of recommending that Graham not be dismissed from the constabulary, citing the fact that the vicar of Whalley and 'others' had written to them expressing an opinion that Malcolm Graham was the best policeman in Whalley and should be spared the sack. They went on to say they trusted that this

Old police station.

Whalley pubs – the Swan Inn shown middle of photograph.

Ruins, Whalley Abbey.

case would be a warning to him and that in the future he should remember, 'Nothing but the greatest necessity could warrant a policeman to strike at any person when taken into custody'.

Lunatic at Large (1919)

In June 1919, the Ribble Valley police were alerted to the fact that a 'lunatic' also known to be a 'common criminal' had escaped from Whittingham Asylum after stealing a staff uniform. The man, fifty-year-old Martin Power, then robbed the railway booking office at Whalley and an engine driver saw him walking along the tracks at about 4 a.m. the next morning.

PC Kay doggedly tracked Power for two days, before arresting him at Edisford. When informed he was wanted in connection with a robbery the escapee told him, 'Yes, that's right: the booking office. I am Martin Power. I escaped from Whittingham Asylum a few days ago, and it was in order to get a public trial that I committed the robbery so I can prove I am not insane'. He added that he had intended to do a few more 'jobs' in the area before he was caught, and admitted responsibility for a burglary at Clitheroe Co-op several years earlier. Power was brought before the magistrates at Whalley Police station, who sent him back to the asylum.

WHIPPING POSTS

Whipping was a method of punishment stretching far back into history. The Anglo-Saxons had knotted cords that they tied together for this purpose.

Right: A Whipping post/pillory/stocks combination.

Opposite: Booking office buildings, Whalley station.

In 1530, during the reign of Henry VIII, the 'Whipping Act' came into being. This declared that vagrants should be tied naked to a cart, and whipped until blood flowed. The vagrants had then to take an oath to return to their place of origin. This act remained in force until the latter part of Queen Elizabeth I's reign, when it was revised. The revision got rid of the cart, substituting a whipping post in its stead, and declared that the subject should now only be naked from the waist up.

A later statute, in 1791, banned the whipping of women, but the public flagellation of men continued for many years.

WHITEWELL

Whitewell lies in the Hodder Valley, close to the old Roman road between Manchester and York. It was once flanked by a royal hunting forest and game bird shooting has long been a tradition in the area.

A Diabolical Outrage (1874)
I have taken the following story direct from the pages of the *Preston Guardian*, because the interest of the tale is as much in the way it is written as in the 'diabolical' events it describes.

> An outrage, or rather series of outrages, of a most fearful and diabolical character have recently occurred at New Hey, Whitewell near Bolton by Bowland. They are of such a nature that had there not been the most undeniable and overwhelming evidence of their truth, it would be difficult that such things could occur in England. The whole neighbourhood for miles around has been in a state of intense excitement and the affair has created a most profound sensation. The Corporation of Preston are at present engaged extending their waterworks at New Hey by utilising the water from the rivers Langden and Haresden. Upwards of 200 navvies are engaged on this work and huts are erected for the accommodation of the men. A man named George Holden took a large farmhouse nearby and lodged between 30 and 40 of these men. From what we have learned by visit, and from eyewitnesses, the life led at this huge lodging house was of the most primitive and uncivilised kind. Before any man retired to bed he had to pay 3d and

he had to pay for his food before he got it. Holden also sold beer without a licence and had as many as 20 or 30 barrels of beer on the premises at one time. We have been informed that women who were not of the most exemplary conduct were also kept on the premises.

On the 11th inst. Holden had to go to Preston on some business and on the Thursday following, his wife went after him, leaving the place in charge of his father-in-law and the servant. During the absence of Holden, strange rumours were heard that the bailiffs were coming and that Holden had eloped the Preston Corporation. The men commenced drinking hard on Thursday and continued until Saturday, entirely neglecting their work. On Friday the men commenced to indulge in a series of orgies of the most diabolical description. In the meantime, the young women, after a series of indecent and strange escapades, went no-one knows where. All this time the men were drinking, there being 20 barrels of beer on the premises. Some of the men went and filled buckets with beer and visited the men who were in bed and asked them to sup. Some did so quietly and others refused. Those who refused had the ale poured over them.

The drinking then became fearful. As daylight broke over the peaceful and rural scene outside, yells and screeches reached the ears inside. Finally the men, being mad with drink and rage, commenced to smash the house and its contents. Doors were wrenched off the hinges, pots, pans, glasses and windows, window frames and furniture were all smashed. A valuable eight-day clock was kicked to pieces. Boxes were smashed open, £20 was stolen; wearing apparel, bedding and furniture were thrown out of the windows. The premises were literally flooded with beer. The men drank beer out of pots, basins, buckets, chamber utensils, dolly-tubs and finally one inventive genius brought a wheelbarrow. The men sang a comic song composed a few days previously. A number of men rushed upstairs and seized hold of a man who was lying sick in bed. They dragged him out of bed, stripped him and brutally kicked him downstairs. He was left lying on the floor with his leg broken and he now lies in a bad state in Preston Infirmary. Holden's father-in-law, an old man, apparently over 60 years of age, was thrown on the floor and a stalwart brute resumed to batter his head with a pot and swore he would kill him. Fortunately he was rescued before life was extinct. The men stripped themselves naked and went into the fields where they fought. There was a steep incline near to the house, and the drunken fellows rolled down the field and were scarcely able to crawl. After rolling 30 or 40 yards, the men became frantic, and the one known as 'Wild Fire' was about to set fire to the premises when he was stopped by the gangs.

Words cannot describe the fearful state of things. The horrible cursing and the beastly conduct that ensued baffles all description. The orgies that were indulged in were fiendish and if we dared shock our readers by describing them, they would be scarcely credible. When the fury of the men had somewhat spent itself, some neighbours went and knocked the heads of the barrels of beer in, and let the beer escape. Some notion may be formed of the amount of beer consumed when we state that we counted 37 empty barrels.

Holden was going to return on the Saturday night but he was informed if he did, he would lose his life, so wisely stayed away. His wife however had more courage and went to the farm but when she saw the state of things she made the best of her way from the place and happily without injury. Most of the men engaged in these horrible proceedings, went away on the Sunday and have not been heard of. The total damage is estimated at £90.

We were informed that a short time ago one policeman had the courage to go to the place but he was stripped, tied to a tree, and a man stood near to him waving a large bowie knife and threatened to rip him open if he spoke. On Sunday last, 5 men were locked up on suspicion of having been concerned in the matter.

Afterword

Crime has always been a feature of human society and although the nature and direction of crime alters with the changing society in which we live, it is likely that this will ever be the case.

Crimes such as returning from transportation, barratry (the offence of frequently stirring up quarrels by spreading false rumours and prosecuting lawsuits), and witchcraft no longer make the court columns of our newspapers but have been replaced by such modern-day crimes as credit card fraud and identity theft. Murder, robbery and even piracy continue, but as social ethics change so do the ways in which we punish our criminals and barbaric punishment spectacles such as stocks, pillories and ducking stools have long since disappeared.

Another change, which has taken place over the years, is the language and style used to report crimes in the media. In 1844, the *Preston Guardian* and *Advertiser* had a code that they printed next to the name of every person they reported appearing at Preston Quarter Sessions: 'r and w im.' meant 'reading and writing imperfect; 'neither r nor w' meant that the defendant could neither read nor write, whilst 'sup' indicated that the person had a superior education. In the same year's publications, I found reports where one Richard Holgate (found drowned) was said to have 'been of weak intelligence'. Richard Nott (assault upon a female), was described as 'a ruffianly looking creature', and Sarah Jolly, 'a poor looking insane creature' was sent to the house of correction for one month for 'constantly annoying' the family of a local butcher.

The reports were often written in dramatic and occasionally sarcastic manner, and although their content is undeniably of a serious nature, the means of their presentation gave me a few chuckles during the research of this sombre and sometimes grisly subject. I leave you with such a report.

Craven Herald, 14 March 1885

ATTEMPTED WIFE MURDER. – On Thursday morning, Thomas Gallagher was committed for trial on a charge of unlawfully wounding his wife Catherine. The parties went to bed together on Tuesday night, and about two hours afterwards the wife was awakened by something sharp piercing her forehead. She screamed 'Murder,' and called for her sister to get up and open the door. The prisoner then said, 'Yes, get up, and bring the bobbies; I have stabbed her with a fork. You said you would have me rotting in prison; you will have your wish now. Give me one kiss before I go.' He stabbed her six times about the eyes with a fork, inflicting serious injuries. The superintendent of police said the prisoner evidently thought at the time that he had done more mischief than was actually the case.

Other local titles published by The History Press

The Prison Service in Britain
BEVERLEY BAKER AND LAURA BUTLER

From the days when prisoners worked out their sentences at the crank, in the silence of solitary confinement, the changes have been vast – as recorded in this fascinating photographic collection. Featuring archive images of prisoners and 'screws', incarcerated mothers and formidable governors and the cells and schoolrooms where inmates passed the hours, the book records every aspect of prison life, providing a unique insight into the history of the penal service.

978 07524 4190 0

Murder & Crime in Lancashire
MARTIN BAGGOLEY

Lavishly illustrated with contemporary illustrations, this fascinating selection of tales of murder and manslaughter from across Lancashire spans more than 200 years of criminal history. The crimes are as diverse as the locations in which they were committed, and include mass murder and suicide in Salford, infanticide in Manchester, a wager that turned to vicious assault in Liverpool and a sweetheart shot to death in Southport – making this a shocking and compelling account of the Red Rose county's darker side.

978 07524 4358 4

Lancaster and the Lune Valley
DR D.J. ALSTON

This fascinating collection of more than 180 old photographs traces some of the many changes seen in the historic city of Lancaster and the beautiful countryside that surrounds it. Spanning the last century, all aspects of everyday life are recorded here, from shops and businesses to churches and schools. Providing a unique insight into Lancaster life as it used to be, the book will appeal to anyone who's ever lived in this city.

978 07524 3007 2

Murder & Crime in Nottingham
ADAM NIGHTINGALE

Explore the darker side of Nottingham's past with this chilling, thrilling selection of true-crime stories. Winding through shadowed side streets and twisting back alleys, the book documents a wide range of murderous misdeeds, from the infamous career of Charlie Peace – master criminal and virtuoso violinist – to the exorcism of Thomas Darling. Featuring cases of sorcery and rioting, gun battles and gaol breaks, it is sure to horrify and captivate anyone interested in the city's criminal history.

978 07524 4496 3

Visit our website and discover thousands of other History Press books.

www.thehistorypress.co.uk